MW00637986

After 40 years in therapy, What have I learned?

WHY WE DO WHAT WE DO & WHAT TO DO ABOUT IT

by

NORMAN C. DASENBROOK, MS, LCPC

PSYCHOTHERAPIST

- Applied Cognitive Behavioral Therapy
- Effective and Assertive Communication
- Creative Problem Solving
- Being Better with Ourselves and Others

Crysand Press

"In between stimulus and response there is a space. In that space is our power to choose our response. In our response lies our growth and our freedom."

Viktor Frankl

Published in 2017

www.counseling-privatepractice.com

After 40 years in therapy, what have I learned? written by Norman Dasenbrook.

ISBN: 978-0-9643949-4-0

Printed in the United States of America

Cover and book design by V2 Marketing Communications, Rockford, IL

Experts Concur

I have worked my entire career (over 38 years) in Sales and Sales Leadership in one of the largest, global and highly-matrixed companies in the world. Throughout my entire career, it has always come down to being able to understand and relate to the people that worked for me, and that I worked with, to achieve a common goal. At IBM, nothing can be accomplished without teaming and consensus. In *After 40 Years in Therapy, What Have I Learned,* Norm lays out the basics of listening and understanding people's viewpoints, and the reasons they might react as they do. He then addresses how to listen and communicate effectively to solve differences and mutually agree to a common goal. This is an insightful and thought provoking book and is a "must read" for all of us that deal with people every day.

Heidi Buchholz
Business Unit Executive, IBM

I've been so fortunate to have Norm Dasenbrook as a mentor and this book shares his wisdom in nutshell! This book provides no-nonsense, practical tips anybody can use to improve their effectiveness in relationships, work and life!

Joyce Marter, LCPC
CEO of Urban Balance

When someone is in successful private practice for 40 years, you can't help but wonder what is the key to their success (and how can I get some?). The book is exactly that — the key to Norm's success! Reading this book teaches you a no-nonsense, practical guide to working with clients. **I loved the "nuggets," specific little gems of advice that will stick with me.** I thought (as you will) "now I am going to remember to use that …"

Francesca Giordano, Ph.D.

Program Director, Clinical Professor,

The Counseling Program

The Family Institute at Northwestern University

618 Library Place, Evanston, IL 60201

A remarkable read that every therapy client should take up before or during therapy. Most therapy books are written by scholars who teach and may have some idea about how real therapy works. Mr. Dasenbrook's book is packed with wonderful ideas, and advice — not platitudes or theory. His forty years of practice in the field shines through as he shows the reader how to use many tried and true behaviors that will be useful to any person that either needs help or has a loved one that does. Dasenbrook takes the reader through five easy to understand chapters that are filled with the wisdom of someone with a longevity in the mental health field. **I heartily recommend this book as a first read before, and during therapy.**

Dr. Jeffrey K. Edwards

Professor Emeritus

Licensed Marriage and Family Therapist

Easy to read and understand. In this day and age when many professionals try to explain complex issues, like human behavior and emotional well being, in complicated terms, Dasenbrook finds a way to simplify it for all readers. "Change your perspective and change your outcome." **Simplicity is the product of genius.**

Calvin C. Williams, MA, LPC-S
Licensed Professional Counselor
HealthPoint Center
1818 Avenue of America, Monroe, Louisiana 71201

From the start, Mr. Dasenbrook engages the reader with a broad overview of psychology and behavior as it relates to everyday interactions. With the use of practical figures and examples, the reader is quickly able to understand fundamental concepts in psychology and apply them to realistic situations. As the book proceeds, a more detailed understanding of concepts is unfolded, making this book user-friendly for a wide variety of professionals. This book reflects the over 40 years of experience gained by the author in mediation, therapy and communication styles. The dissemination of pragmatic information is seamless and easy to digest, making this book a useful tool for professionals in the field as well as those who are not specialists in behavioral health.

Dr. Mini Tandon,
Psychiatrist St. Louis, Missouri

It is an honor to give Norm Dasenbrook's new book my highest recommendation. As Norm, I have 40 years in private practice. I conceptualize what we do as counselors as being teachers. People come to us to learn how to better deal with the issues that are confronting them. Norm is a fantastic teacher. His book is filled with practical and useful techniques to help clients resolve many of the issues they face.

Harvey Kelber, LCPC
Past President, Illinois Counseling Association
Past President, Illinois Mental Health
Counselors Association
Past Chair, Illinois Counselor License Board

Norm Dasenbrook's *After 40 years in therapy what have I learned?* is **a treasure trove of solid techniques, ideas, stories, metaphors, and advice that help us change our lives for the better!** This book brings cognitive behavior therapy down to a molecular level, enabling us to apply it to our daily lives — be it regarding our marriage, family, or work relationships.

Those in business will also find this book helpful in understanding and moving past everyday work hurdles, promoting an open, change-oriented culture. *After 40 years* goes beyond cognitive behavioral therapy to include something often missed: The art of listening. It is so easy to forget how powerful listening is. In this book, we are reminded that it is the essence of human connection, and we are given tools to enhance this connection with others.

Dasenbrook wisely points out how we humans are comfort seekers, which can be self-defeating in our efforts to change and grow. He expertly teaches you how to manage that discomfort so that you can reach goals that may previously have rested just out of reach.

I found the range of topics in this book to be interesting, and will be of interest to many readers. Examples include, self-esteem, relationships, work, love, parenting, conflict, ADHD, anger, and assertiveness. There is something for everyone in this book, and you will find Dasenbrook's multitude of examples extremely helpful to apply the material to life's problems and opportunities.

It is not often one finds a book filled with common sense, but this book includes so much practical application that you will find yourself grabbing it off your shelf over and over. **Better yet—leave it on the coffee table for all to enjoy!**

Lorna Hecker, Ph.D., LMFT, CHPS
Professor, Purdue University Northwest
Hammond, Indiana

What a wonderful and witty break down of dealing with a multitude of mental health issues. I've never had it explained so eloquently, simply and in such an entertaining manner. I have every intention of giving a copy to each of my adult children. It has simple but helpful solutions to some of the basic difficulties of raising children and working with different types of people. A definite must-read.

Susan Peterson
Owner, Personal Best Training

After 40 years of therapy, what have I learned?
Contents

Foreword
The Search for The Holy Grail

A long time ago in galaxy far away, I was a young student at the Tulane School of Social Work. I remember embracing the fantasy: That truly here, I will learn the alchemy of psychotherapy.

I recall many conversations with professors and peers about numerous books and theories that would reveal the "secrets" of therapeutic relationship and clinical intervention. We students searched for the "how to" of changing people's thinking and behavior, and the more elusive skill of converting theory into practice. We sought what to say after you say, "Hello," and other such treatment unknowns. We were on a quest for the various holy grails of psychotherapeutic healing. After New Orleans, that searching process continued throughout my career — not really ending until I hung up all my, "tell me how you feel about that" retorts. I suppose we all do a similar thing.

To this "grail" search I added experience plus the good fortune of meeting-up with a few mentors and gurus who guided the completion of my quest that begun so many years before. Norm and I met during the midst of this quest process. For years he and I learned together, sharing methods and techniques, i.e. secrets and nuggets.

After I retired, Norm continued refining and expanding his grasp of this complex process of intervention into human interaction, collecting more "how-tos" as he went. He wrote books, conducted seminars, and supervised and mentored others. I often thought how fortunate those young therapists are to have met-up with Norm at such a formative place in their careers.

Norm and I have continued our clinical collaboration — between my retirement fishing duties and our joint family activities, due to our "in-law" status. He constantly continues to amaze me with his ability to not only explain to others the "how to" of our business, but to teach the usage of those bold, sometimes subtle techniques, that we all read about, but find the application too often difficult.

This book is a culmination of Norm's career long observations, experience and innate clinical creativity. Read it ... reread it and make it a part of who you are. I wish I could have known its contents a long time ago.

— *Paul R. White LCSW*

Acknowledgments
It's all about relationships

I would like to thank the thousands of clients who invited me into their lives at very difficult times. The therapeutic relationships that were developed in order to help and learn will be forever imprinted on me. It was a privilege to serve my clients. I truly enjoyed going to work every day!

Not only client to counselor but relationships with employees, partners and colleagues influenced and shaped my outlook on life: Office manager Andrea Swanson, RN who worked with me for 19 years, until her passing; Paul White, LCSW who I worked with in private practice for over 25 years. Not only was Paul a partner and mentor he became an in-law when my daughter Jessica married his son Jeffery. Nadia Johnson, LCPC who joined the practice over 11 years ago until her retirement. Le Anne Paulson who has done our billing and dealt with difficult insurance companies. Mike Mastroianni, partner, co-author and one of the best speakers and consultants I have ever seen. Mike and I have enjoyed working together for almost 30 years. Mike authored much of the effective and assertive communication chapter that was written for our book, "Harnessing the Power of Conflict."

In 1997, I attended a meeting of the Illinois Mental Health Counselors Association. I attended that meeting to say, "Thank You" for getting counselors licensed which allowed me to continue my work. Next thing I knew I was chairperson of the professional development committee! I have continued my association with my local and national professional organization ever since as a Board member, consultant, workshop presenter and volunteer with a great group of colleagues. The friendship and mentoring of such fellow counselors as Bob Walsh and Pat McGinn will last a lifetime.

I would like to acknowledge my editors and creative people who helped me organize and communicate my thoughts in proper English: Le Anne Paulson who helped me with sentence structure, punctuation and spelling; Caitlin Walsh who wanted to major in English and be a writer who wound up with degrees in Psychology, Sociology and Criminology.. She is now starting grad school for a masters in counseling. Her fresh perspective was a great asset. Pat McGinn who edited this book from stem to stern and had no problem challenging my chapter layout. So, thank you Pat for how easy this book flows from chapter to nuggets and back again. Kathy Velasco from V2 Marketing who has assisted me in all of my publications for over 25 years with design and format.

Lastly, I would like to acknowledge Heidi who put up with me as I wrote this book. I am ADD, and Heidi (as well as many others) can confirm the diagnosis. She is the love of my life and my best friend.

So, you can see it's all about relationships!

— Norm Dasenbrook

Introduction

40 years in therapy: What have I learned?

Welcome to *40 years in therapy: What have I learned?* People usually don't read the introduction of a book, so I am glad you are reading this and I will keep it brief.

My career in psychotherapy spanned five decades from the late 1970s to the late 2010s. I have spent over 40 years in therapy. Mentors Carl Wacker, Paul White, Mike Mastroianni, Pat McGinn, cognitive-behavioral therapy, conflict resolution/mediation, communications, advances in medications and plain good old common sense have molded and shaped the processes I used to help individuals, couples, families and organizations. I always said that helping others was not overly complicated. Not nuclear fusion. To give back, I would like to share with others whether you are a clinician, spouse, partner, parent, supervisor, CEO, teenager, or regional manager of the universe, what I have found helpful in helping people be better with themselves and others. I have found that most of us, to be the best they can be with themselves and others, need three things.

First, we need a way to understand ourselves and others that's practical, observable and measurable. Why we do and feel the way we do? There are many theories in psychology but I have found that cognitive behavioral theory seems to make the most sense. Simply stated, feelings and behaviors are side effects of how we see the world (perceptions). Change those perceptions, and your feelings and behavior will change.

Second, we need to communicate and listen better. We are not born communicators, and we tend to hear what we want to hear! Most couples that come for counseling cite communication as a major problem. Think about it. If we had a way to express ourselves clearly, and truly listen to others, most of our relationship issues would be solved. The positive and assertive communication techniques I have found and explained in this book, will take your communication skills to another level.

Third, we need different ways to solve problems that enhances our relationships with others. Along with cognitive behavioral theory, effective and assertive communication, I have found mediation techniques that can make even hostile relationships better and good relationships great.

In addition to the three major components of this book, I have added my observations about what people, families and organizations go through in order to change. The Misery Zone and what to do about will help guide you through that change process.

When most people try to change themselves or others, they experience these reactions. I call these reactions "The Misery Zone." When people bump into this misery zone, they go back to the old way, believing change isn't worth the stress it causes.

THE CHANGE PROCESS

OLD WAY

The Misery Zone

Anger	Stress
Frustration	Blame
Fear	Silence
Resistance	

NEW WAY

Go through the misery zone for change to happen

But when you get these reactions from yourself or others, you are half way to the new way. You get these reactions because most changes don't take place without them.

Normally, you don't drive home and say to yourself, "Gee everything is going so well in life that I think I'll go to a counselor and get better." Being uncomfortable is a sign that you are in the change process. It means it's working. If your child has to live with new rules, the child will react when you are beginning to get through to him or her. It means change is happening.

If you remain consistent, the change will occur. Don't give up when you get negative reactions. People react to get you back to the old way, because the old way is familiar and comfortable to them. They knew the "old" you ... they were used to the "old" you. The new way makes them unsure of you.

If you remain consistent, they will change the way they respond to you.

Think of it in terms of a soda machine. If you put money in the machine and don't get your soda, what do you do? Shake or kick the machine, right? Now, if you get the soda you have taught others to escalate their behavior to get what they want. If you still don't get your soda, you eventually walk away. People are the same way ... if they react and you don't give in, eventually they'll get used to the change and all will be fine ...

Change can seem negative and insurmountable; but with patience, it can be a process that revitalizes an organization or family. Since change cannot be avoided, it makes sense to use the best techniques available to make the change easier. Following the concepts of this book, we can minimize confusion, resistance and anger so our work and family lives can function smoothly.

Change can take place from the **inside-out** or from the **outside-in.** We have all experienced outside-in changes ("I'll just throw the pack of cigarettes out and make myself not smoke" or "I'll make myself like her"). Initially, an outside-in change can work, but it is labor-intensive and hard to keep going. Instead of that type of change, or in addition to it, inside-out change works best. If we change what we believe/perceptions, our feelings and behaviors soon will follow.

The information in this book will act more like an antibiotic than aspirin. If you have a headache, you take aspirin and the headache is gone. If you have an infection, you take an antibiotic over and over again to get better. You will need to repeat these over and over for them to work. Consistency over time is how you get meaningful, permanent change.

Also, I have added what I call *Norm's Information* or *Therapy Nuggets*. These "nuggets" are therapy techniques, analogies, metaphors, sayings, common sense pieces, quotes from others, problem solving and communication tips that I have found helpful in my work and I would like to share them with you.

Lastly, I will share with you my "Stay or Go" stress model that can be used to, as what Kenny Rogers sang about "Know when to hold 'em and know when to fold 'em."

To best illustrate the essence of this book, I have included the letter below. This couple was able to employ the three major components of this book:

Understanding Human Behavior: Cognitive Based Model

Effective and Assertive Communication

Problem Solving: Mediation

It transformed their lives and the lives of their children. They had taken court ordered co-parenting class, and as a result changed their perceptions subsequently their feelings and behavior. She and her ex-husband learned how to communicate and problem-solve in a respectful manner that truly transformed their family.

To Whom It May Concern:

My now ex-husband Chris and I were court-ordered to take the Co-parenting Class instructed by Eileen McCarten and Norman Dasenbrook.

I would like to share a bit of our history and explain what a turning point the class was in our lives and that of our children. Chris and I were in divorce court for over 2½ years. About an hour into our first mediation session we were asked to leave and told there was no reason to come back for the additional sessions because there was nothing she could do for us because we were both so absolute on our positions.

Our divorce was as unpleasant as everyone else's. We were stuck in a rut of accusations and inability to communicate in any way without it erupting into a very ugly argument. I was at a point to where when my email or text notification went off with his ringtone it made me physically sick. Often times I wouldn't even read what he had sent. We used the children to transport items between us and often times to communicate for us "tell daddy ..." I avoided all conversations with my children about their father when they would ask questions. We only attended the same events when we had no other choice. We sat on opposite sides of the room at their events, in school and outside of school. We made no eye contact.

Our kids would ask why we wouldn't say "hi" or "bye" to each other. My then 6-year-old at one point asked why mommy and daddy hated each other so much. We communicated through our GAL instead of to each other. We went through all the drama of saving every single text in case you could use it against the other person later and choosing your words so carefully so that they couldn't do it to you, making it virtually impossible to have any sort of effective communication about our children. We did not enter each others homes we sat in the car and let the kids take themselves to and from the door carrying their bags and belongings.

The effects our behavior was having on the children was detrimental and obvious. They were stressed out. They felt insecure. It affected their sleep, their schooling and their overall mental health. We were stressed out and I know for myself the effects of the stress caused me to be very short-tempered with my children and time I should have been spending with them was spent digging through ten years of emails looking for "that one time he said …"

I alone spent $137,000 in attorney's fees between the *Guardian Ad Litem* and my own attorney.

In November we were court ordered to take the class. We had "homework" we had to do prior to the first co-parenting class and part of it was reading and watching videos of children talking about how much their parent's horrible divorce affected them. The whole time I was watching I was thinking to myself "I know, I know, but I am a great mom and I love them so much they'll be fine."

After the very first actual class I realized that my children were in fact NOT fine no matter how much I loved them. We went through basic communicating skills, decision making, problem solving and throughout the entire 4-week-class the entire focus was about actually co-parenting our children. Not just parenting unilaterally as a dictator and not caring how their father did it when it was his time because in my mind clearly I was so superior as a parent.

I realized that very first day that our children's entire childhood was going to be solely defined by our divorce and all of our adult issues and no matter how wonderful I was with them or he was with them, the memories they would have of their childhood wouldn't be all of the wonderful times we had, it would be the animosity between their parents. Because at the end of the day children need their parents on the same page in order to function themselves. They need them to communicate and be amicable.

I, like most parents, say I will do anything for my children. I will walk through fire. Take a bullet. Kill for them. But could I swallow my pride for them? Put my love for them above my feelings for their father and rise above to give them what they needed?

The class showed us how to do exactly that. It started slow. Forcing ourselves to at least say "hello" when we saw each other at events. And when the kids noticed and would comment "wow you and dad said hi to each other," I was so ashamed of my behavior and how it had affected them and how long I let it go.

We wasted years of our children's' childhood with our own selfish, petty behavior. Spent thousands and thousands of dollars that should've been spent on them.

I believe 100% that if the Co-parenting class had been ordered in the beginning we could have saved all that time and money for our children. We listened and we learned how to put our children first and how to effectively communicate. We have come a long way. It was baby-steps but little by little we continued to use the tools we learned in the class and are able to offer our children what they deserve from divorced parents. It's hard enough for them to live in two separate homes without adding all the drama on top of it.

We are able to share a meal and both attend our children's birthday parties, even when it's at one of our homes. We always greet each other and can even talk and laugh with our kids together. I credit the class completely for where we ended up.

Hopefully the legal system will see this class as a top priority and realize that the success this class has proven to have is a vital part in keeping families on-track and their children as the main focus.

Thank you for your time,

Chelsa

—CHAPTER ONE—

Understanding Human Behavior

Cognitive Behavior Therapy — Explained

CHAPTER ONE
Understanding Human Behavior
Cognitive Behavior Therapy — Explained

In any human interaction, it is helpful to have some way of understanding ourselves and the behavior, thinking, and feelings of others to comprehend how we are relating to each other. Many of us make assumptions about why people behave the way they do, but few truly strive to understand. What defines an individual, a family, culture, religion, corporation or society? Moreover, without a framework for understanding, we lack an effective strategy to understand, grow, influence or change.

Understanding human behavior and interaction is obviously not an easy task. Since the beginning of time people have tried to explain why we do what we do. Greek and Roman philosophers debated the essence of man. Epictetus wrote in the "Enchiridon" that "men are disturbed not by things (events), but by the views which they take of them." Centuries later, Shakespeare in Hamlet wrote, "There's nothing either good or bad but thinking makes it so."

When Sigmund Freud began documenting his work, the general population became interested in psychology and human interaction. He explored such concepts as the conscious versus the unconscious, and the id, ego and super ego. Ever since Freud, a number of schools of thought and theories of psychology and human interaction have arisen.

Alfred Adler, a noted psychiatrist in the 1930s,

documented the same thoughts of Epictetus, other Stoic philosophers and Shakespeare, saying that a person's behavior springs from his ideas. He said that a person relates to the world based on his own *interpretation* of himself and his present problem and not by anything predetermined. He also noted that *attitudes* determine relationships to others and the outside world. Everything depends on *opinion.*

In the 1950s Albert Ellis founded what he called Rational Emotive Therapy, or RET (now called REBT). Basing his thoughts on those of others before him and fueled by his growing dissatisfaction with traditional approaches to understanding human experience, Ellis found that peoples' *beliefs influenced their feelings and behaviors* more than events of the outside world. (Corsini, 1973).

In the 1960s Aaron T. Beck, a psychiatrist, noticed that thoughts were not as unconscious as Freud had previously thought. Moreover, he hypothesized that certain types of *thinking (automatic thoughts) led to dysfunctional behavior.* It was from this hypothesis that Beck developed cognitive therapy (now called cognitive behavior therapy or CBT). A person's core beliefs, according to Beck, can affect mood and behavior.

The main idea behind CBT is that the thoughts and beliefs of individuals, families, work groups and societies affect how they operate in very powerful ways. Mistaken beliefs and negative thinking can both contribute to and maintain negative behavioral patterns, interactions, and even mental illness (Sexton, 2003). CBT works to change negative thought patterns into reality based ones that result in positive, constructive behavior changes.

So let's take a closer look at how this cognitive based model can be used. Stated simply, we must not focus on feelings, behaviors or positions but on the *perceptions* and needs that give rise to those feelings, behaviors and positions.

Most of us are familiar with the Stimulus/ Response model of human behavior. In the presence of a certain stimulus, a specific response is elicited (show a dog meat and it will salivate). This theory has been applied to people and work groups (reward a job well done, and people will be proud and will work harder).

STIMULUS

RESPONSE

In our daily lives, most of us feel that the Stimulus/ Response concept is true. How many times have we said things like:

"You're making me crazy."

"You make me angry when you do that."

"You make me feel worthless when you criticize me."

"Everyone wants to quit because you make it miserable around here."

"You don't do your share of the work, and it makes me sick."

"I can't stand being around you anymore."

These statements indicate that an outside event causes a feeling in a person, or one person's behavior causes a feeling or action in another. What Shakespeare, Adler, Ellis and Beck found is that this is not necessarily true. They discovered that something happens between the stimulus and the response that causes the feelings and reactions. If this were not true, then why would the same stimulus elicit different responses in different people? For example, a wage freeze may cause one to feel happy ("I'm glad I still have my job and there wasn't a layoff,"); another to feel angry ("I'm not making enough now as it is,"); another confusion ("What's a wage freeze?"); and still another indifference ("Who cares? What else can they do to us around here?").

In families when a child gets caught in a lie, some parents might yell ("This is just horrible,"); others may be passive ("I'm sure she didn't mean to,"); while others may lecture ("She needs a good talking-to,"); or others may sit down and talk with the child ("We need to find out what's going on.")

SAME STIMULUS

DIFFERENT RESPONSES

The model actually looks more like this:

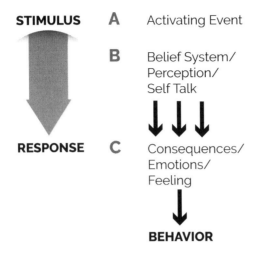

What takes place between the stimulus, or event, and the variety of responses or feelings is a third factor called the belief system, self-talk or perceptions.

It is helpful to view this in the framework of the Rational Emotive Therapy Model of Albert Ellis. Ellis looked at the stimulus as an activating event (labeled "A"), the belief system as perceptions or self talk (labeled "B") and the response as the feelings or emotional consequences (labeled "C") (Corsini, 1973).

Following this model, the perceptions (B) and not the activation event (A) cause the emotions (C). Keep in mind that once we feel, the feelings drive our behavior.

The following illustrates the concept, in sequence:

A	**(Event)**	Winning the Lottery
B	**(Perceptions)**	"No financial worries." "Our boat has come in." "We can put the kids through college and retire in style."
C	**(Feelings)**	Happy / Euphoric
	(Behavior)	Quitting my job.

As you can see, it is not the event (A) that causes the happiness/ euphoria and the job resignation; it is the perception of financial security that causes the feelings of happiness, and those feelings drive the behavior (quitting).

At work, the same model applies. For example: If your supervisor were to walk into your office and say, "I need to see you in my office pronto!" and then abruptly walk out of the office, how would you feel? Most of us would look at the events, perceptions and resulting feelings as follows:

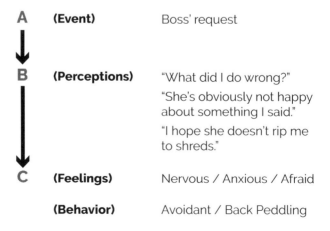

A	**(Event)**	Boss' request
B	**(Perceptions)**	"What did I do wrong?" "She's obviously not happy about something I said." "I hope she doesn't rip me to shreds."
C	**(Feelings)**	Nervous / Anxious / Afraid
	(Behavior)	Avoidant / Back Peddling

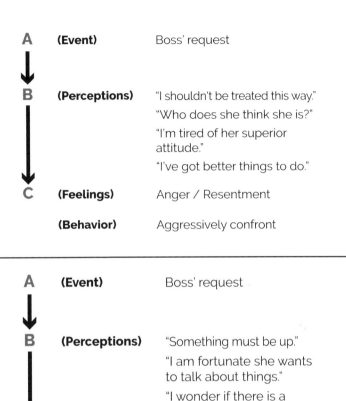

A   **(Event)**   Boss' request

B   **(Perceptions)**   "I shouldn't be treated this way."
                          "Who does she think she is?"
                          "I'm tired of her superior attitude."
                          "I've got better things to do."

C   **(Feelings)**   Anger / Resentment

     (Behavior)   Aggressively confront

A   **(Event)**   Boss' request

B   **(Perceptions)**   "Something must be up."
                          "I am fortunate she wants to talk about things."
                          "I wonder if there is a misunderstanding."

C   **(Feelings)**   Calm / Rational

     (Behavior)   Problem Solving

Was it the fact that the supervisor walked into your office that caused these feelings of anger, frustration or nervousness? The answer to that question is no. What caused the feelings *is what you told yourself* about why the supervisor was in your office.

The perceptions (B) drive the feelings (C) and the subsequent behavior. The events (A) do not cause the feelings. This explains why people can react differently to the same event or situation. Have you ever felt different emotions about the same event? In accepting a job promotion or transfer you might feel excited, yet slightly scared or apprehensive. Why? Because you are telling yourself that it is a compliment to be promoted or transferred, but it is new and unknown.

The same model applies at home as well. Let's look at an example of a child's lie again:

A   **(Event)**   Child's lie

B   **(Perceptions)**   "This is just horrible."
                           "If she lies about this, what
                           will she lie about next?"
                           "We can never trust her again."
                           "How dare she lie to <u>us</u>?"

C   **(Feelings)**   Horrified / Angry

      (Behavior)   Yell and scream
                           at your daughter.

A   **(Event)**   Child's lie

B   **(Perceptions)**   "Well, we're going to put a stop
                           to this right now."
                           "Just who does she think she is?"
                           "We haven't raised a liar."
                           "She certainly needs to
                           be set straight."

C   **(Feelings)**   Indignant / Betrayed

      (Behavior)   Lecturing /
                           Talking down to her

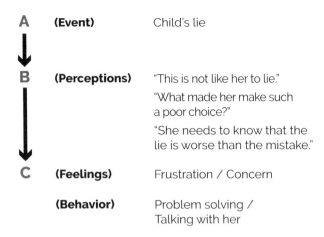

Our belief systems/perceptions/self-talk drive our behavior. If I believe that I am getting put down by a sarcastic comment from you, even if you didn't intend it to be so, I may feel angry; and my resulting behavior might be either a verbal attack, ignoring you or walking out of a meeting. The belief system/perception/self-talk causes my behavior. If you don't understand my belief system at that point, you might be totally shocked by my behavior.

So it is clear we need to look at our own perceptions, as well as those of others, to understand why we feel and behave the way we do. Perception is the engine that drives the train. Feelings and subsequent behavior are the caboose. They are side effects or by-products of our perceptions. If you had pneumonia and were coughing, I could give you cough syrup and you would cough less. But the disease or pathology would be left untreated. **We need to deal with perceptions and not feelings if we want to change behaviors.** This is not to say that feelings are not important. Although feelings should be acknowledged, it is in the perceptions where a person has the greatest chance of influencing behavior.

Where do perceptions come from? Perceptions are made up of values, morals, past learning, gender, ethnicity, education, traumatic events, other life events, parental messages, current events and our life experiences. They are the lenses through which we see the world. Sometimes the lenses are distorted. If they are, we see the world in a distorted fashion. Everything is filtered through the belief system, our perceptions or what we tell ourselves (self-talk). This is how we evaluate the events our lives. If our lenses (perceptions/self-talk) are skewed even 10 degrees right or left of center (reality), then our feelings and behavior will be equally skewed 10 degrees right or left of center (reality). And if the perceptions are grossly inaccurate, the resulting feelings and behaviors will be grossly inaccurate, as well. While there are many ways we can see reality in a distorted fashion, there seem to be four primary critical perception errors that can negatively impact our feelings, behaviors and our interactions with others.

PERCEPTION ERROR #1: POLARIZATION

The first of these errors is called polarization. This is the tendency to view reality in polar opposites (sometimes referred to as "either-or thinking"). Some examples of the polarized thinking include:

The list can go on.

We learn these polarities early on in life. If you weren't a good little boy or girl growing up, what was the only other option? Probably bad or naughty. Rarely did your parents come home and say, "My, you are so mediocre today!" If you attempted something new, you either succeeded or you failed.

In adulthood, the same polarizations are still evident in most of us. We have a good boss or a bad boss, we have a good day or a bad day, or a good evaluation or a bad evaluation. When our belief systems are locked into wrong or right, good or bad, yes or no, then our feelings and behavior will follow accordingly.

If we see events in the polarities, our feelings and behavior will swing wildly as a result. A person who has extreme mood swings is on an emotional roller coaster; way up one minute and down the next. Again, this is a result of perception polarization, not changing events. If you work with or have a relationship with someone who is on an emotional roller coaster, you get to go on the ride for free.

In reality, events are usually shades of gray. They are matters of degree, and few of them are absolute. If we can shift our thinking and see life as a continuum rather than as a series of polar opposites, we can experience many more emotional and behavioral options–options that are more reflective of reality.

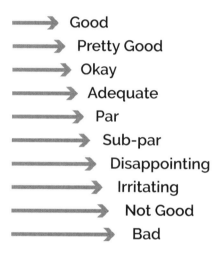

Good

Pretty Good

Okay

Adequate

Par

Sub-par

Disappointing

Irritating

Not Good

Bad

We are doomed to polarities unless we choose to alter our perceptions and see the world for what it is. This is not to say that we need to look at everything as wonderful—the "power of positive thinking" idea. I'm not suggesting that you think of yourself as a flower waiting to bloom or see each day as a growth experience. I call that the art of positively lying to yourself. It reminds me of the old advertisement about, "Is the half a glass of water half full or half empty?" Don't know about you, but to me, it's just half a glass of water (reality). You can dress it up and say, "The glass is half full", or dress it down and respond, "The water is half gone." Or if you have ever been through a downsizing or rightsizing at work, you could say," You know what? We have twice as much glass as we need!" The point is that we need to view things as they are. If we do, we can avoid escalating a mildly frustrating event into a nuclear disaster, thus expending more much anger and energy than is warranted. This is not to say that bad or awful events just don't happen; they do. But I challenge you to wonder if they happen with the regularity that we see them.

PERCEPTION ERROR #2: AWFULIZING

This brings me to the second critical error: awfulizing, or the skewing of emotions that labeling causes. When we "awfulize" to extremes, feelings and behaviors again will follow. Have you ever said to yourself, "This is the worst possible thing that could have happened to me. It's horrible!" Or, "Why did this happen to me? What did I do to deserve this?" If we talk to ourselves like this, labeling events as awful, horrible, terrible or catastrophic, how do we expect to feel? Perky? It isn't going to happen. You are going to feel awful, horrible, terrible and catastrophic and will behave accordingly. And you will be miserable to be around.

What do you want on your tombstone? Crabby? Intense? A pain in the ass? The one at work who always tried to shoot down new ideas? Unless you come back as a bird or a rock, you only get one shot at life. There's no do-over. This is no dress rehearsal. I see so many people who get up in the morning already feeling overwhelmed and under-appreciated. They get themselves to the office and have a to-do list for the day that could not be accomplished in a week. They get home and see that the house is a mess, feeling no one else helps out. The dog threw up. They cook dinner, pay the bills, go to bed and wake up—only to do it all over again.

Again, the beliefs or perceptions cause the feelings and resulting behaviors. To avoid awfulizing, we need to watch the words or labels we use to evaluate our life events. We need to ask ourselves, "Is this really bad, awful or horrible?" Some events are. If so, go ahead and feel terrible. But terrible events rarely happen weekly, daily or hourly, unless we choose to see them that way. Ask yourself, "Is it awful, or is it merely a pain? Is it disappointing or irritating?" A nuclear war that destroys society is the worst possible catastrophe—everything else is an inconvenience.

Where does this tendency to awfulize come from? Let's pick on childhood; as a child, if you got four As and one D on your report card, what did you spend dinner talking about? We seem to be oriented toward the negative in order to fix it, but we seem to shy away from what's going well and celebrating it.

In my clinical practice, I have had many clients who saw their accomplishments as, "at least I didn't screw it up," or as "dodging bullets." When they perceived themselves in this manner, they would feel relief or moderate anxiety, but never really good, excited or satisfied. When they were able to accurately see their accomplishments for the successes and triumphs they were, then and only then could they feel successful or triumphant. Many counseling clients that suffer from depression will admit to awfulizing or at least minimizing events in their lives in an effort to not feel too good, assuming that the better they feel, the more likely a negative event will occur ("Just like when I start to feel better something always comes along to knock me back down"). If they were feeling too good, they would really crash hard when the next bad thing happened. Not true. Simply stated, if we perceive badly, if we label awfully, we will feel poorly. The alternative is to believe in the continuum, which drives behaviors in a much more real way and which gives us more choices.

PERCEPTION ERROR #3: SELF-DEPRECIATION

The third critical error is self-depreciation. If our self-esteem were measured like oil in our cars, many of us would be a quart or two low (some people wouldn't even register on the dipstick.) This low self-esteem can be turned inward. This type of self-talk sounds like:

"How can I be so stupid?"

"I really am a screw-up."

"What did I ever do to deserve this?"

If my self-esteem is low, I may feel responsible for how others feel and behave. If someone is upset, I may turn on myself and wonder what I did to cause that feeling in them ("It must have been me"). Or I might say, "Let me apologize now for the mistakes I will make in the future." But really, you're not so powerful that you can cause others to feel and behave in ways they don't choose. Turning on ourselves leaves us few options for change and lots of opportunities for victimization, and the resulting inaction, depression, unassertive behavior and non participation. If we think we are inadequate and terrible and a failure again, the feelings and behaviors surely will show it. Eleanor Roosevelt once said, "No one can make you feel inferior without your permission".

Sometimes self-depreciation can show itself in the downplaying of accomplishments. Some people can't seem to take a compliment. I hear, "Oh it was nothing" or "It's no big deal really; anybody could've done it." With just a couple of self-defeating perceptions, they totally negate the reality of the compliment, don't feel special and fade into the woodwork.

The opposite reaction to this way of thinking can also be toxic when we blame and project our low self-esteem or problems on everyone else rather than owning some of the responsibility ourselves. The resulting feelings will be hostility, aggressiveness and grandiosity. "The VP is cheating us again... The supervisor is out to get me... They don't realize how valuable I am to this company."

These are the people who chronically feel like they get the short end of the stick. Nothing is good enough, fast enough or fair enough. If you said, "My it's a nice day," they would respond, "Yeah, if it doesn't rain." If they won $1 million in the lottery, they'd say something like, "It's a rip-off. You don't really win a million dollars. You only get $750,000. The state takes $250,000 for taxes. They're a bunch of liars. Why don't they just call it the $750,000 lottery and be honest about it? If I had known that, I wouldn't have wasted a buck on the lousy ticket." These people can be very unpleasant to be around.

PERCEPTION ERROR #4 OVERGENERALIZATION

Ellis, in his landmark publication, "Guide to Rational Living," and Dr. Burns, author of "Feeling Good" , both describe a perception error of overgeneralization. This occurs when we use such labels as always, never, can't, have to, ought to, must and should.

Always, never and can't represent a negative experience in the past that is generalized as a never-ending pattern now and projected into the future. Perceptions such as, "I always seem to screw things up," "I never get what I really want," or "I can't seem to do anything right" are just not true. At some point in life—today in fact—you have accomplished something without making a mistake (arrived at the office without crashing your car?) Day in and day out most of us get our needs met (nourishment, socialization, shelter, etc.) And every day we do things right (tie our shoes, make a phone call, get to where we are going). Granted, everyone makes mistakes: We settle for something less than what we want, and we have times where things don't go as planned. But is it really an ongoing, never-ending life pattern? If you think this way, you will feel defeated, anxious and unmotivated.

Have to, ought to, must and should are labels we use

in an attempt to motivate ourselves—for example, "I have to do well," "I must succeed," "I should do more." These statements produce unnecessary pressure and resentment. Ellis once called this musturbation, and self-help groups refer to this as "shoulding" on yourself. When we label events in this fashion, we become apathetic, unmotivated and set up for failure. Moreover, when we apply labels to others, such as, "He shouldn't treat me like that," or "I have to be treated with respect," we become so resentful that others can't reach our level of expectations.

These examples show the problems associated with perception errors and illustrate how much our own self-talk drives our feelings and behaviors. The good news is that we have a lot more control over these things than we think we do. We may have little control over the activating events (A), but we have plenty of control over the perceptions (B) and thus can influence our feelings (C) and our resulting actions. If we can listen to where others are coming from, we can influence the feelings and resulting actions from them, as well, through constructive confrontation and mediation.

The cognitive based model presented here has use not only for understanding others but also ourselves. Rather than looking at events, behaviors or situations, we need to focus on perceptions and belief systems in order to understand others and ourselves. Although we may have little or no control over events, we do have control over our beliefs and perceptions. We can choose how to view them.

If we want to change how we feel or behave,

we need to change how we perceive events and situations. Since we cannot control our co-workers or family members, we can at least control how we respond to them. We can examine how we are viewing situations to see if they are accurate.

Most people will say they are aware of the events that occur in their lives, as well as their feelings and behaviors: but they're not sure if they are really aware of their perceptions or self-talk.

An event can occur, and we immediately feel something and respond quickly. Like when you're talking to your 15-year-old daughter, and in the middle of the conversation, she rolls her eyes and says, "Whatever!!" You probably get instantly crazy and say or do something you later wish you hadn't. That is the power of association. Over time we learn, in a healthy or unhealthy way, to respond to certain events in a predetermined manner. But somewhere along the line, thoughts (self-talk) or perceptions must occur. We all have our buttons; when they're pushed, we respond.

To find out what our own perceptions or self-talk are, we need to talk them out or write them down. Get them out of our heads and expose them to reality. Thoughts in our heads are like an endless loop that just goes around and around like a dog chasing its tail or a run-on sentence. But when perceptions are spoken or written, they become straight and linear. Then and only then can we evaluate them to see if they reflect reality.

Have you ever been in an argument with someone and realized that what you were saying was wrong, but you kept on arguing anyway? Or have you ever been reprimanding your child and realized you sounded just like your own mother or father (and you had sworn to yourself you would never sound that way)? It's because you got your thoughts out of your head and you heard them for the first time. This is why it is important to talk with a friend, spouse, counselor or co-worker, to get the perceptions out so they can be evaluated.

Another idea is to keep a journal or diary so you can see your perceptions. I suggest writing something simple, like the following:

A. Event (What happened?)

B. Perceptions (What am I thinking or saying to myself about the event?)

C. Feelings (What am I feeling?)

Over time, patterns of perceptions will emerge, indicating whether any of the critical thinking errors are present or if some other form of distortion is occurring. Once we identify how we are perceiving events, we can choose to change them to better reflect reality or conclude that they do reflect reality and proceed.

I hope this gives an insight into self and others and perhaps explains feelings and behavior. For ourselves, if we see that our perceptions are distorted, we can change them and thus change how we feel and behave. Again, it is not the power of positive thinking. We are not saying that a person should perceive bad things as good, as if a nuclear bomb dropping really is a mere inconvenience. What we are saying is that we can get along with others better when we see that everything isn't awful and catastrophic and that everything is not worth 100 percent of our energy. If we see the world as it is—not in black or white, but in shades of gray—we will not overreact. If we understand perceptions as a way of trying to understand feelings and behavior, we'll have a much stronger foundation for better communication and problem solving.

As you can see, feelings and behaviors are side effects of perceptions. They are by-products of our thoughts. Since we have the most control over our perceptions—not events, feelings or behaviors— we need to focus on perceptions to be effective communicators and problem solvers.

Feelings and behaviors are clues to you as you interact with others. If someone is way up and down emotionally, you can predict that they are polarizing. If someone seems to be angry and irritable, they might be awfulizing. Likewise, if someone seems apathetic, unmotivated or avoidant, they could be self-depreciating or over-generalizing. You need to listen for and verbally challenge those distorted perceptions to help them see the event more realistically.

In the early 1990s, I was asked to consult on helping a dysfunctional work group. Along with a partner we applied the concepts of CBT to work with our first client company and found great results. We thought that workgroups were similar to families and suffer from the same pathology. As such, we used the cognitive model as our frame of reference to help transform the culture. It made so much sense to us, that we taught the cognitive based principles to the employees. It was a model that made sense in the boardroom as well as the loading dock. Once the self-defeating perceptions and cultural roadblocks were identified, employees were able to help define a new culture (set of desired beliefs) that produced better results. And we have been refining our approach to cultural change ever since.

In my first book, "Harnessing the Power of Conflict: Optimum Group Performance Through the Self-Mediation Method," Mastroianni and Dasenbrook, 1994 we documented our process of helping dysfunctional work teams using these concepts along with action planning, communication training and codes of conduct. More recently, the effectiveness of the cognitive model was well documented in the book "Change the Culture, Change the Game" by Connors and Smith, Portfolio/Penguin 2011. They found that, "The power and persistence of the culture (perceptions) explains why the usual tactics that mangers use to improve results often don't work. Most of the fixes, from new people and new technology to new strategies and new structures, only work at the level of actions (behaviors), when they work at all. Too often leaders attempt to change the way people act without changing the way they think (i.e., their beliefs). As a result they get compliance, but not commitment; involvement, but not investment; and progress, but not lasting performance."

Ignoring the culture (perceptions/belief system) and focusing on actions or behaviors doesn't work. In training executives and managers in how to deal with underperforming employees and conflicted situations, I usually ask, "What's your strategy, methodology or game plan on how to approach and potentially deal with this type of situation?" Most look at us like deer in the headlights, stunned and frozen. For they realize that they do not have a well-crafted and theoretically sound approach.

In fact, if they have an approach at all, it is behavioral in nature. Reward or incentives will cause people to work harder. What we and others have found is that incentives are only a small part of cultural change. For example, if the employees think the morale at work sucks and management decides to give a 2% raise, that doesn't necessarily change anything, because the employees think, "Great, now I make more money at the place that sucks". Or an employee of the month program is started where the employee of the month gets to park right next to the building. Most employees would think, "Great, now I can get to the place that sucks quicker." The cognitive based model is the basis of our work in changing cultures, improving individual performance, communication, problem solving, coaching and action planning.

Again to quote Connors and Smith, in the book "Change the Culture, Change the Game" they state: "There is a simple yet powerful relationship between the beliefs people within the organization hold and the actions they take. If you change people's beliefs about how they do their daily work and help them adopt new beliefs you want them to hold, you will produce actions you want them to take."

Norm's Nuggets

These "nuggets" are therapy techniques, analogies, metaphors, sayings, quotes from others, common sense pieces, problem solving and communication tips that I have found helpful in my work. I would like to share them with you. In this chapter I have included the following nuggets:

NORM'S NUGGETS

Therapy Nuggets: Depression, Anxiety & ADHD

THE CHANGE PROCESS

OLD WAY

The Misery Zone

Anger	Stress
Frustration	Blame
Fear	Silence
Resistance	

NEW WAY

Go through the misery zone for change to happen

From the introduction, I have included the THE CHANGE PROCESS here because it is very important to implementing all the nuggets and because some of you didn't read the introduction.

So when most people try to change themselves or others, they experience these reactions. I call these reactions "the misery zone." When people bump into this misery zone, they go back to the old way, believing change isn't worth the stress it causes. But when you get these reactions from yourself or others, you are half way to the new way. You get these reactions because most changes don't take place without them.

Normally, you don't drive home and say to yourself, "Gee everything is going so well in life that I think I'll go to a counselor and get better." Being uncomfortable is a sign that you are in the change process. It means it's working. If your child has to live with new rules, the child will react when you are beginning to get through to him or her. It means change is happening.

If you remain consistent, the change will occur. Don't give up when you get negative reactions. People react to get you back to the old way, because the old way is familiar and comfortable to them. They knew the "old" you...they were used to the "old" you. The new way makes them unsure of you. If you remain consistent, they will change the way they respond to you.

Think of it in terms of a soda machine. If you put money in the machine and don't get your soda, what do you do? Shake or kick the machine, right? Now, if you get the soda you have taught others to escalate their behavior to get what they want. If you still don't get your soda, you eventually walk away. People are the same way ... if they react and you don't give in, eventually they'll get used to the change and all will be fine ...

The techniques, analogies, metaphors, communication tips and nuggets in this book will act more like an antibiotic than aspirin. If you have a headache, you take aspirin and the headache is gone. If you have an infection, you take an antibiotic over and over again to get better. You will need to repeat these over and over for them to work. Consistency over time is how you get meaningful, permanent change.

A-B-C Journal

The purpose of this homework exercise is to help you recognize the thoughts/perceptions that influence your feelings and behavior. To find out what our own perceptions or self-talk are, we need to talk them out or write them down. Get them out of our heads and expose them to reality. Thoughts in our heads are like an endless loop that just goes around and around like a dog chasing its tail or a run-on sentence. But when perceptions are spoken or written, they become straight and linear. Then and only then can we evaluate them to see if they reflect reality.

Sometimes events happen and you just react. That's the power of association. In order to understand and ultimately change some of our perceptions, we need to separate the events from the perceptions and the feelings.

So, as events occur write down what happened (activating event) and the feelings (consequences). Then go back and write down the thoughts (perceptions) that caused those feelings.

A Event

B Perceptions

C Feelings

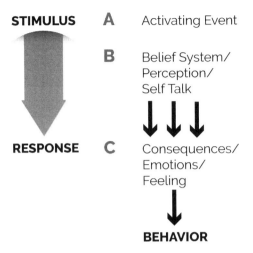

Examples 1 & 2 show how two different perceptions (B) about the same event (A) cause two different emotions/feelings and behavior. As events and feelings occur in your life, write them down and then write down the perceptions/thoughts using the A-B-C model.

Example 1:

A	**(Event)**	Child's lie
B	**(Perceptions)**	"This is just horrible."
		"If she lies about this, what will she lie about next?"
		"We can never trust her again."
		"How dare she lie to us?"
C	**(Feelings)**	Horrified / Angry
	(Behavior)	Yell and scream at your daughter.

Example 2:

A	**(Event)**	Child's lie
B	**(Perceptions)**	"This is not like her to lie." "What made her make such a poor choice?" "She needs to know that the lie is worse than the mistake."
C	**(Feelings)**	Frustration / Concern
	(Behavior)	Problem solving / Talking with her

A

B

C

A

B

C

All the lights can come on (insight) but you still need to find the door (to do step).

A lot of clients begin counseling wanting to know "why do I do what I do?" They want some insight or concrete explanation that they can believe explains why they do what they do! As therapists we have ideas, theories, psychological testing, hunches and the like, but at this time we don't have the diagnostics that other helping professionals possess. We don't have an X-ray, CT scan or MRI device where we can say, "Ah, ha..see here the pink spot that's what is causing your depression, anxiety, OCD, ADHD or bad attitude. We make assumptions. Even if we could be 100% sure why you do what you do, you still need a plan on what to do about it. Just because all the lights come on, you still need to find the door.

Did the alligator come in the front door or back door? Time for alligator removal.

Depending on the severity of the symptoms, sometimes we need to do symptom reduction before we look for causation. At times, I tell clients it doesn't make any difference if the alligator came in the front door or the back door. It's alligator removal time. Later we can go back and figure out how the alligator got there in the first place.

1st thought 2nd thought.

Over time if we suffer from low self-esteem, depression, anxiety, OCD or ADHD, we can develop automatic thoughts that are somewhat skewed or distorted. These automatic thoughts (B) cause the feelings (C) not necessarily the event (A). The automatic thoughts are the 1st thoughts and can be challenged (and over time replaced) by 2nd thoughts that are more reality based. Below is an example of an A-B-C journal entry from a client who has an anxiety disorder. You can see (and so did she) that her anxiety was exacerbated by all the questions in (B). She was able to challenge or reframe those thoughts with more reality based statements. Over time the 2nd thoughts start to become the 1st thoughts and reduced the symptoms.

1st thought

A. There is a cut on my gums.
B. What is it? How did it get there? Is it infected? Is it oral cancer?
C. Scared, worried.

2nd thought

A. There is a cut on my gums.
B. The mouth usually heals fast.
It's most likely not serious.
C. Reassured, neutral.

ADHD 1st thought 2nd thought

One complaint from parents (and teachers) and partners about kids and husbands with ADHD is that they seem to lie about little things. I think it is more about being impulsive and having automatic thoughts to please or to avoid consequences. "Is your homework done?" Response is "Yes" (1st thought) while the kid is thinking: " Do I have any homework? Where is my history book?" Oops! Now he can't take it back and continues to lie. Or the husband who promises a friend his help to move on Saturday and impulsively says 'yes' to his wife's request for time on Saturday and has to lie to someone to correct it. I suggest to the kid, parents and partners to ask for the chance to give the question a second thought without consequences (and the chance to delay the response) to say, "Yes, history, but I'm not sure if I have my book."

Reverse 1st thought 2nd thought overthinking

Now there is usually an exception to every rule, and here is one. Some people with depression or anxiety over think their issues and ignore their first thoughts, which seem to be pretty much reality based. Just listen to yourself or someone who does this, and you will hear, "I do a good job at work, but I just feel like I'm under a microscope, and if I make one wrong move I'll be gone." Or, "My boyfriend didn't text me back right away. Is he pissed? What did I do? He always texts me back immediately, why not this time? OMG … Did he do something?

Next time just go with, "I do a good job." Or, merely, "No immediate text."

Anger management?

Why manage something you can prevent? It has always amazed me that the "field" of anger management has gained as much traction as it has. People go to anger management counseling, attend groups, even get ordered to it by the court. It never made sense to me to manage something that was preventable. Anger is a side effect, a byproduct of distorted perceptions. Over time, anger can become a conditioned response to certain stimuli, but it is a learned response that can be unlearned. Change the perceptions and you change the feelings!

Power of association

If a friend shows you a piece of candy and hits you in the head with a 2x4, over time you learn to duck! You don't pause to think….candy, wood, pain, what should I do? No, you automatically duck. That's the power of association. Your brain associates the candy with a bad outcome and automatically responds by having you duck, as it should! But, the power of association can work against us. If you have a panic attack or heightened anxiety in the grocery store, going over a bridge, in an elevator, or in a crowd, you could associate the place with the anxiety and think about avoiding those places. But those places didn't cause the anxiety; it was what we told ourselves about those places and how we felt.

One day upon entering the shower I saw a big spider in the corner. It shocked me because I never saw a spider in the shower. So, for the next month I looked in the shower first for spiders before I got in, even though I had gone in that shower a thousand times with no problem. It only took one time for me to question the possibility of spiders to change my feelings and behavior.

Butectomy

People have a tendency to discount themselves or accomplishments by using a but. "Thanks for the compliment, but anybody could have done this."

"I hear what you are saying, but I could never do that."

"That might work for others who have depression, but not for me."

What comes before the but gets discounted or negated, and what comes after is felt. If you need to do a butectomy, put in a period and start a new sentence. Another example is those 'yea, buters," who seem to be agreeing with you, but after the but, tell you why they discount what you are saying.

Crisis is opportunity

Few people change unless there is a jolt or crisis. The trouble is, if we handle crises poorly, we'll get the same poor results crisis after crisis. Each crisis needs to be approached (perceived) as an opportunity to do things differently—maybe better—and should not be dreaded and avoided. Every crisis is truly an opportunity to solve problems in a way that potentially enhances the relationship, not one that damages it.

Need to remember you have a remembering problem.

All of us have something we struggle with. Those of us who do it better, acknowledge our issues and plan accordingly. With ADHD kids (and some adults), I work with them to remember that they have a remembering (focus, distractibility, concentration) problem. For example, when standing in front of their locker, they need to think, 'I need to remember I have a remembering problem,' so they can refocus on what they need to bring home for homework. It is just a fun refocusing technique that works in a variety of situations.

Power of 3s.

A great remembering technique is the power of 3s. Most tasks or processes can be broken down or remembered in three steps. Especially with ADHD kids this gives them a structure. They need to think, "what were the 3 steps for _____?" Now it seems counter intuitive to have a kid remember 3 steps as opposed to one thing, but it works. For example, what are the 3 steps for homework? Could be:

1. *Bring home subject material and complete the assignment.*

2. *Put it in my back pack.*

3. *Hand it to the teacher.*

It is easier to remember all the steps than just do the homework. The last step is so important as parents always complain that their kid forgets to turn it in. I say the homework is not done until it is in the hands of the teacher!

—CHAPTER TWO—

Effective and Assertive Communication

CHAPTER TWO
Effective and Assertive Communication

There is no escaping conflict or confrontation, whether in the boardroom, bedroom or family room. At times it seems that we just float from one conflicted situation to another. Whether this is due to our contemporary, fast-paced lifestyles or global warming is not known. What we do know is that most of us AVOID conflict and confrontation, or we save up conflicts and cash them in when we reach the final straw, generally ripping the other person to shreds and feeling guilty ourselves.

Most of our inability to handle conflict originates from our past experiences in handling difficult situations or people. Let's blame childhood. How many confrontations did you win with your parents while growing up? What would have been the likely response if you said to your mother or father, "Mom… Dad, I've polled my brothers and sisters and we have a list of ten demands on how you need to change." You probably would not have heard, "Yes dear, you're right, we do need to change." You may have heard something more like, "Just who do you think you are to talk to me this way? Go to your room!" How many confrontations did you win with teachers, traffic cops, customer relations people, or supervisors? If we're honest, we have to admit most of us have a negative perception or belief when it comes to successfully dealing with conflict.

The good news is that there is plenty we can do to effectively confront people and manage conflict. All it takes is applying some common sense and adhering to a few basic principles.

Here are those principles:

To effectively and assertively express yourself, you first need to own your feelings and behavior. As I earlier quoted Eleanor Roosevelt, "No one can make you feel inferior without your permission." No one nor event can cause you to feel or behave in any way that you do not choose. We cannot control events and other people, but we can control how we feel, and we can take ownership of our reactions.

If we do not accept responsibility, we will likely communicate in "You messages." We will say such things as, "You make me so angry;" "You are driving me crazy;" or "You make me feel so worthless." These are blaming statements to which most people do not respond in a positive fashion. These kinds of statements won't elicit a group hug or an invitation to dinner.

If we do accept responsibility for our feelings, we'll make statements more like, "I feel angry when you don't communicate with me, because then I think the relationship is one sided;" or "I feel worthless when you talk to me that way because it puts me down." This is an assertive way to communicate how you feel and how you see things. It is not insubordinate or necessarily antagonistic. While some spouses, peers, co-workers, bosses and children may respond with something like, "I'm sorry, that's not what

I meant;" or "I didn't mean to hurt your feelings," other people may get defensive...which leads to the second principle.

Most problems can be solved by simply listening and truly trying to understand the other person. But most of us don't do that. We are so driven to get our point across or to defend or explain ourselves, we get lost in our own heads. Our objective should be to understand the other person, whether we are being confronted or whether we are confronting someone else.

If your eight-year-old says, "You don't care about me. You spend all your time working or cleaning the house," you could respond in a number of ways. Such as, "Well, sometimes I don't feel like you care about me, either;" (fighting back) or, "Mommy has been very busy;" (rationalizing) or, "Oh, come on now, you know I spend as much time with you as I can;" (minimizing) or, "I'm doing the best I can;" (defending).

Instead, next time listen and respond with a statement that indicates that you do understand, for example, "It sounds like you're feeling left out;" or "It seems that you think I'm not spending enough time with you."

Before you can be understood, you must first seek to understand. Let the other party speak first and truly try to understand, though not necessarily to agree, with them. Stephen Covey once said, "Most people do not listen with the intent to **understand**. Most people listen with the intent to **reply**. "Then you can give your side. If you confront someone and they react, allow them to talk until they are finished before you continue. Ask questions to ensure they get it all out. Then they will be more receptive to hear what you have to say."

Now keep in mind that there is a big difference between *understanding and agreeing* with someone. You may feel that you are spending all the possible waking moments you have with the child, but getting that point across to the child is not what is *initially* important. What's important is that your eight-year-old feels heard and that you understand the child's feelings. Then, and only then, can you solve problems and generate options if necessary. Perhaps just hearing the child's concerns will be enough.

Listening will solve 50% of the problems. Most people just need to be heard and acknowledged without someone jumping in and telling them what to do. Listening benefits more than the listener; it allows the speaker an opportunity to hear his or her own perceptions, as well. Besides, you just might be persuaded if you truly listen to the other side.

The same principles apply if you're doing the confronting. Let's say you need to tell the boss that your work is stymied when she doesn't get back to you with decisions in a timely fashion. You may say, "Ms. Smith, I need to tell you I feel confused when you don't get back to me, because then I am unsure how to proceed." She may respond with, "I get back to you as fast as possible. I have other priorities around here, you know;" or "You know, you might need to be a little more independent rather than always relying on me."

At this point you will need to fight the natural tendency to use the four letter F-word ... and say "FINE" and walk away. Also, you need to fight the urge to get defensive or to over-explain your position. Here again, just like with your eight-year-old, you need to communicate your understanding, not necessarily your agreement. Responses such as, "I am sure you have multiple priorities and are very busy;" or "You're feeling that I lean on you too much for direction?" indicate that you understand and are willing to listen. Even if you reflect back the wrong feeling or sentiment the other person will simply correct you. If, for example, your partner says, "I wish our sex life was more spontaneous and daring," and you respond, "So, you think I'm dull in bed?" if this is not what your partner intended, he or she will correct your interpretation. It will sound something like this, "No, all I'm saying is we need to spice things up a bit;" or "I'm not feeling that you are dull, it's just that things seem to be getting a little routine."

Mike Mastroianni points out in *Harnessing the Power of Conflict* that some may feel that this process is "techniquing" people or parroting. It is not. "Techniquing" people occurs when you reflect back everything a person says or you reflect only the content of what was being said and not the feelings. If a co-worker were to call you a weasel, you wouldn't want to ask, "So, you think I'm a small burrowing mammal?" Responding to the feeling with, "It seems as though you feel angry with me," is much more appropriate. Likewise, if the boss was discussing her vacation in the Bahamas and said, "Man, my trip to the Bahamas was great!" a techniquing response would sound like the following:

"You went to the Bahamas and it was great?"

"Yeah, we spent all our time at the beach." (boss)

"You spent all your time at the beach?"

"Well, not all our time. We visited some of the shops." (boss)

"You went shopping too?"

"Oh just forget it. What's wrong with you?" (boss)

"You want me to forget this conversation and are concerned about me?"

If you did this, people would think you truly had gone over the edge. One of many possible responses that would not be "techniquing" or parroting the boss, could be, "Your vacation sounds like it was just what you needed."

Now that the person feels understood, you can:

1.) Get back to the point of the confrontation.

2.) Stop the discussion if listening was sufficient.

3.) Try problem solving if necessary.

Whatever communication strategy you use needs to nurture or enhance the relationship and not damage it. If you are not listening, but instead are trying to get your two cents in first, win the argument or become aggressive, you can expect that it will damage the relationship. If you think in terms of winners and losers, everyone loses. What good does it do us if I win and you lose when we still need to live or work together?

The majority of communication happens in the context of an ongoing relationship. Always keep in mind that preserving the relationship is equally important to getting your point across. Demonstrate your concern for the relationship by listening, asking questions and trying to problem-solve. Don't treat the communication process as a contest. If you win at the other party's expense, you damage the relationship, which means everyone involved effectively loses.

However, if the relationship has no value to you, go ahead and do whatever you want. Let's say you're in a remote city that you probably will never visit again. You go through the drive-up window at a fast food restaurant and get shorted your cheeseburger. In a remote city, you could ask, "Do you remember birth?" while you pull the kid's head through the little window. However, in your hometown, this would not be advisable because we know what they can do to your food when they know you and don't like you.

The same logic applies to business or family relations. Our primary objective is to enhance relationships — getting away from winners and losers — because we have ongoing relationships with those in our business and family. This approach addresses the problem and does not attack the person. Once the relationship is secure, then and only then will you be able to communicate your point of view and/or problem solve.

Attack the problem, not the person. Verbally attacking the other party only increases their defensiveness and escalates their emotions. Even if you feel that they are attacking you, don't retaliate. It serves no purpose in problem solving to lower yourself to critiquing personalities. Separating the person from the problem allows you to concentrate on solving the problem, not on the other person's personality. Whether or not you like the other party, problem solving is not a game to see who can get the best of the other.

In order for you to be heard after you have attempted to understand the other person, an empathy statement can be very useful. Going back to your eight year old, you could say, "I can understand that at times you feel like I don't care about you because I'm busy, but I do love you and want to spend as much time as possible with you. I just wish there were more hours in the day to fit everything in." With the boss, an empathy statement might sound something like, "I can appreciate that you have a full plate. All I'm saying is that the quicker I get a response from you, the more efficient I can be," or, "Perhaps I could be more independent: I just want to do the best job possible without trying to assume I know what you need." Even if you disagree with the other person's opinion, first show that you understand and then give your point of view. Remember, it's the quality of the relationship that is important.

There are no magic formulas in handling conflict or touchy situations. All too often our emotions get in the way and we wind up creating a bigger problem. Stephen Covey once said, "Common sense is not common practice," and it definitely applies here. Hopefully, you can find some common sense in accepting your feelings and behavior and can work on understanding before you are understood, to enhance your relationships.

Confrontation or leveling

We don't always learn the proper ways to communicate assertively. Regrettably, there wasn't a class on this in grade school. The word "confrontation" conjures up fear and trembling with most people … probably because most people didn't exactly win most of their confrontations in the developmental years. In addition, we probably haven't won many later in life. So our track record isn't good, and even if we learned how to confront, it still seems uncomfortable because of our negative experiences.

Here is the first opportunity to use the art of changing perceptions, self-talk or belief systems. Here is the opportunity to view confrontation as a relationship building and nurturing experience.

What do I mean by that? Doesn't confrontation usually lead to anything but relationship building or nurturing? Actually, the opposite is true. If we never express our feelings and subsequently our perceptions to others, they will never have an opportunity to explain their actions, apologize, defend their position to us, or problem solve with us. We will never have the opportunity to work it all out. And if we never tell someone that what they are doing is hurting us, themselves, or others, we are guilty of passive approval, that is, we condone the behavior and enable it.

For example, let's say someone is making disparaging remarks about a person you like. You say nothing. Likely the person making the remarks will believe you agree, and in fact, has every right to believe you agree. So, the person making the remarks continues to make them, which hurts the friend. By confronting the situation, many people's feelings can be spared. The offender may learn a valuable lesson about gossip, and may think twice before speaking about someone in an improper way next time.

Confrontation is essential to preserving an on-going relationship. It is not the "yelling at each other" or "arguing" that we may have experienced as a child. It is problem solving at its best. If the relationship is to be preserved, confrontation at some point will be necessary. It may not be necessary to work at a relationship that is NOT on-going. But, if we want to nurture an on-going relationship, we will need to "talk it through," or confront the other person at some point in time. When we engage in actions that hurt the relationship, we may find it will not be on-going for long. Actions that hurt the relationship include angry outbursts (when you can't take it any longer), keeping silent and keeping it all inside, (pretending everything is OK., when it isn't), or yelling — just to name a few. Confrontation does not include any of these things. Confrontation is not yelling. It is assertively communicating, expressing needs and listening to the needs of others in order to problem-solve.

Mike Mastroianni said, "There is, obviously, a right and a wrong way to confront someone." You can say, "You have a face that will stop a clock," or you can say, "When I look at you, time stands still." In either case you get your message across, but the first way may get you in more trouble than the second. Although confrontation takes us out of our comfort zone, the process that follows should make it easier.

Let us assume that you wish to modify the behavior of another person, or at least how that person interacts with you. Before you start, be sure you understand the problem. Be clear on what your issue is. And pick the mountain you want to die on … that is, confront only on the issues that are most important to you. Take a stand on the hill that is worth defending. You wouldn't want to waste a confrontation on a minor issue; doing so may further deteriorate a relationship, as the person may feel that you are making mountains out of molehills.

When economic inflation occurs, our dollar becomes worth less. Too many dollars, and they diminish in value. In a similar manner, too many confrontations, and they, too, diminish in value. Be clear on which important issue you wish to discuss.

Begin the conversation with an "I" message. Do not begin with flattery, or small talk ("My what a lovely tie," or, "Isn't it cloudy today?"). These messages dilute the impact of what you are saying.

"I" messages usually can be worded as follows:

I think _____ .

I need_____ .

I feel _____when you_____
because _____ .

Examples would sound like:

I think we should save money for our vacation.

I need the toys picked up from the driveway now.

I feel angry when you don't pitch in because then I have to do more than my share of the work.

Contrast this with typical "You" statements — accusing statements that use the word YOU.

You always spend our money right before we need it for our trip.

You brats pick up those toys now before I really get mad.

If you would get up off your ass and help me, maybe I'd get out of work on time for a change ... don't be so lazy.

I guarantee that if you use the "YOU" message, the people you are confronting will not jump to their feet to apologize and do what you ask with a smile on their faces.

When "I" messages are used, the focus is placed on how a person's behavior impacts you. Make sure you deal with what is happening and do not attack or use labels. Labels (you are lazy, shiftless, you have a bad attitude, you are careless) hurt too much to help and are likely to trigger more anger and defensiveness. Be careful not to send a hidden attack disguised as an "I" message:

"When little brats don't pick up their toys, I get angry and need them picked up."

"If certain people would quit being so lazy, I wouldn't have to work so hard ... I need cooperation."

As you can see, there is a subtle slam, sandwiched in between these "I" statements. It will still evoke a negative response from the recipient, who will more than likely hear only the attack and not the "I" statement.

After sending an "I" message, the person receiving the message will still be defensive, and may elect to justify, rationalize, blame, defend, withdraw, use humor or minimize so as not to have to "own" the "defensive feelings." We all sting when receiving negative feedback, no matter how constructive the intention. So if we don't like receiving criticism we can imagine that neither do others. Expect defensiveness...then, if it doesn't occur, you can be pleasantly surprised.

A person may either get quiet, accept the feedback, or attack back. In any case, it is important to acknowledge the feeling, and "pull it through," so to speak, to get to the person's perceptions. It is a temptation at this point to "play in the feelings area" and get angry and defensive when someone else is being defensive with us. If we let that happen, we may find ourselves in a heated argument instead of a problem-solving confrontation. In order not to play in the feelings--in order to get to the perceptions which you can influence--you must "jujitsu" through the feelings; that is, acknowledge the feelings and pull them through. Unlike street fighting where force is met with force, jujitsu is a martial art where force is met with a step to one side, and the pulling through of the person, using their own force to knock them down (Fisher 1988). Often we can jujitsu a person's feelings out of the way in order to get to their perceptions by merely using "You" messages. "You" messages are listening statements. "You" messages can be of three types: passive listening, active listening, and empathetic listening.

Passive listening occurs when nothing is said, and a response of "uh huh" is typically given as the most verbose response. The sole purpose of passive listening is to let the other person continue to vent or speak. It lets them go on without your interruption, or comment. It draws quiet people out and helps them to feel comfortable enough to continue.

Active listening is useful only when clarification of content is desired. If we are unsure of what the other person is saying, we can reflect back what we heard in order to more fully understand their thinking.

(You think_____ .)

Empathetic listening is the most useful method, where the feelings of the other person are reflected back in order to get to the perceptions.

(You feel _____ .)

Sometimes people don't even know what they are saying, because the message is mixed in with such intense feelings. When you acknowledge a feeling with a "You" message, you do three things:

1. You clarify the feeling.

2. You keep yourself from reacting and thus starting a war.

3. You show the other person that you heard the feeling, which calms the person down and allows you to get into the area of perceptions so that you can problem-solve. Ninety-nine percent of the time, a simple "You" message will catapult a person right to their perceptions. And once we are dealing with perceptions, we can influence behavior more easily.

An example would be:

("I" message) "I'm sick and tired of having so much work to do and having no help."

("I" message response) "Aw, don't be such a martyr … you sit on your ass once in awhile just like the rest of us, so don't go getting in my face about how you do all the work."

("You" message) "So you feel that I'm nit-picking, and that you are doing your share of the work?"

("You" message response) "Yea … we all work hard, and I'm pissed when I get accused of being lazy."

("You" message) "You think I'm attacking you and saying you're lazy."

("You" message response) "Well, maybe you don't mean it that way, but that's sure how it sounds."

Notice how the tone begins to get less hostile after a couple of "You" messages. It settles things. It also keeps the person who is confronting from getting angry and arguing back to defend her or himself. If the "You" message weren't used, the exchange might have sounded more like this:

("I" message) "I get sick and tired of doing all the work around here and getting no help."

("I" message response) "Aw, quit being such a martyr ... we all sit on our asses once in awhile, and besides, I get sick and tired of you getting on your high horse and attacking us."

(No "You" message used) "Me ... what about you ... you can't even work for the whole shift ... and how dare you accuse me of sitting on MY ass ... "

"Aw, get away from me, there's no talking to you ... you're not the boss."

"If I were the boss, I'd fire a lazy idiot like you."

"Oh yea ... wanna take it outside?"

This time, the problem escalated into a possible physical confrontation.

Even reflecting back the wrong message is OK. Remember, "You" messages also give us an opportunity to clarify ... if we get the message wrong, they will just correct us. For example, if someone said,

"Boy, some of us are really in a foul mood today."

And you said,

"So you're not having a good day."

They will probably say,

"No! I'm referring to you. You seem to be the one in the bad mood."

Empathetic listening seems to be more effective at diffusing anger than active listening. Here again we can see that responding to the feeling is more powerful than responding to the content.

When attempting to use "You" messages effectively, we must resist the temptation to be negative. Let's say, if your partner comes home from work and says, "I can't stand that place anymore ... I'd like to quit."

An example of an effective "You" message might be:

"You feel angry about work" (feeling), where the partner will likely respond, "Yea, the boss criticized my report again." (perception)

Notice how the partner goes right from feelings to perceptions. Now you can discuss things, problem solve, or merely listen, whatever seems called for. If you were to use the negative alternatives, your responses might have been ineffective and have sounded like this:

(order) "You better not quit ... we need the money."

(warn) "If you do, you may not get a job like that again."

(preach) "I felt like that at my job. I just told the boss where to get off, and she backed off after that. I think a person like that boss needs to get a lesson on self control."

(advise) "Why don't you just tell the boss to go pound sand."

(criticize) "Can't you handle that jerk yet ... you've been there for four years and we go through this every other night."

(teach) "Practice it with me ... I'll be the boss, and you tell me where to get off."

Sometimes we might even interrogate, which we think is actively listening, but can be frustrating, and may escalate the person's anger. ("What did the boss say ... did you tell her where to get off ... does she pick on all the people or just you ... how is Myrna handling it?) Remember, the objective is to listen and not respond yet.

"You" messages can be used after you confront someone if they get defensive, or you can use them to help you keep control if you are being confronted by someone else.

For example, if you were at your desk and someone came in and said, "You never answer your messages, and I really needed to talk to you ... that makes me mad."

(You could respond:) "You are angry because you needed to get a hold of me and I didn't return your call."

After sending "I" messages and "You" messages-- and after the person has calmed down and has told you what her or his perceptions are — then it is time to begin to restate your position and express your needs. Normally, this begins with an Empathy Statement, such as

"I can appreciate how you'd feel _____."

"I can understand how you could think that _____."

"Hey, I'd feel that way too if I thought that _____."

followed by:

"But all I'm saying is that I need _____."

Either the person will move into discussion with you, or you can just listen if that is all that is needed. If they are still angry, you can continue to use "You" messages and Empathy Statements until they are calm enough to continue, or until you deem it necessary to end the conversation. Even if it isn't all settled when you end the conversation, at least the person will have heard you, and you can leave without carrying the anger or stress of unfinished business around with you.

A complete exchange might go something like this:

"I'm sick of you not doing your share of the work. We've all been talking and everyone thinks you need to work harder."

("You" message) "What you're saying is that I've been sloughing off."

"Yeah ... we all worked an extra weekend and you didn't volunteer. That pisses us all off."

(Empathy Statement) "And I can appreciate how that would look to all of you. If I thought someone was getting away with murder, I'd be pissed off too."

"We aren't saying you did it intentionally ... but we'd like it to be fair."

(Empathy Statement) "I can appreciate how you want things to be equitable ... so do I. All I want is to have a schedule that is fair, but one where we get some notice in advance. My weekend was scheduled and we were going to be out of town. What you all don't know is that I told the boss I'd do two next month since I didn't do any this month."

"We didn't know that ... but I'm sure everyone will understand now. Look, let's just drop it. Don't feel bad about bringing it up to me ... I'm glad you did. I would rather talk about it than to have people talking behind my back." (Mastroianni 2003)

Remember that the purpose of this method is to open channels of communication, but a more important purpose is to PRESERVE THE RELATIONSHIP. What's the use of winning the battle if you lose the war? Confrontation such as this can actually nurture the relationship, as it did in the example above. Both parties now have a better understanding of each other's behavior, and have been honest and open in the process.

Sometimes it's not what you say but how you say it. If my 17 year old wants a new car and we can't afford one, I can say, "Don't talk to me about the car ... I don't want to hear about it." Or I can say ... "I can understand that you feel like your old car isn't very nice, and I'd like to be able to get one for you, but I'm afraid we'll have to wait a while."

Who would you rather talk to next time you have a problem? I'd go to the person who listened to me. It is important to understand that I need to hear you before you will have any desire to hear me.

What has been talked about can be summarized as follows:

Constructive Confrontation or Leveling

1. I need _____.
2. You feel _____.
3. I can appreciate how you'd feel _____, and

I'd probably feel that way too if I thought_____;
but all I'm saying is that I need _____ or we need

_____.

What are some examples of successful confrontation or leveling?

Let's look at some opening statements in different circumstances that may help you begin the leveling process.

To describe poor work performance to an employee:

"Mary, I've noticed that you haven't been meeting the performance standards. I need to have all team members meet at least the minimum standards."

To talk to a supervisor who reprimanded you in front of your peers:

"Bob, I've been thinking about the verbal reprimand the other day, and I felt embarrassed that others heard it. I wish that could have been done in private."

To talk to a child about a bad report card grade:

"Sue, I had hoped you'd pass all the subjects in school. I want to talk to you about how you can improve your math grade next quarter."

To talk to a parent about an undeserved punishment:

"Mom, I know you are angry at me for not coming home before curfew, but I feel two weeks grounding, including not being able to go to Homecoming, is harsh."

Practice framing the opening sentences in implied or stated "I need" messages. Depending on the reaction, the conversation can go in many directions, but remember:

• Know your hot-buttons so you don't lose control. If you feel out of control, just say, "I'm getting angry, so I'd rather talk when we can both be calm."

• The relationship is of the utmost importance. Don't sacrifice the relationship to make a point.

• Use "I need" or "I feel when you _____" messages as openers, either stating those words or implying them.

• Watch the barbed-wire words. Watch the tone of voice and facial expressions, like laughing or smiling, when someone is leveling with you or when you are communicating something serious.

• Use "you feel____" to show an understanding of another's feelings.

• Use empathy statements, such as "I can appreciate how you feel _____" when you understand someone's perceptions. (Mastroianni 2003)

Finally, know that a failed attempt at leveling does not mean the process didn't work or that you screwed up. The attempt helps to preserve the relationship. Just trying the process will help show people you are making an attempt at understanding them. It will pay off.

Norm's Nuggets

These "nuggets" are therapy techniques, analogies, metaphors, sayings, quotes from others, common sense pieces, problem solving and communication tips that I have found helpful in my work. I would like to share them with you. In this chapter I have included the following nuggets:

NORM'S NUGGETS

Communication Nuggets: Tips

If someone is bitching or gossiping too much, someone is listening too much

There is a difference between venting and complaining. If someone is complaining and you passively listen, they have every right to think you agree with them (passive approval). You don't have dumpster written on your forehead. You can say you aren't comfortable listening to that, and perhaps redirect the person back to the source. (Mastroianni 2003)

H-A-M: Hear it – Acknowledge it – Move on

People have a fundamental need to be understood. You know how it feels when you feel understood by a friend, partner or family member. They "get or feel" you, and it feels quite nice. You also know when you don't feel understood. Understanding someone is not the same as agreeing with them. I can understand you and think you are from Mars. But, I can listen to you and acknowledge what you think and/or feel and move on.

Best time to talk about a problem is when it is not occurring

In the heat of the moment we are not usually at our problem solving best. Sometimes it makes sense to revisit an issue later. This is especially true when you can sense things are going bad and only going to get worse; you can call a time out. Saying something like, "We are getting nowhere with this," or "I can feel myself getting frustrated," or "Let's stop now and talk about this later." If we agree ahead of time that a time-out is OK, we can call for one, but make sure the issue gets discussed later and is not avoided.

Volleyball: Don't go for the kill shot (point) too quickly

Sometimes we try and get our point or position (kill shot) across too quickly. People have a greater likelihood of listening to you if you first listen to them. Just like in volleyball, you have to set up the point with a couple of passes (listening) first, then attempt to score (make your point)

Mediate not Litigate

Legally or metaphorically, don't give away your decision making power to others. My colleague Paul White was always telling his adolescent clients, "If you don't manage your life, someone else will, and you won't like it." When individuals, couples, and families look to others to solve their problems or tell them what to do, chances are the decisions don't meet the needs. Give people a process, a language, a sense of hope and empowerment, and most will rise to the occasion. I was a divorce mediator for over 20 years and a collaborative law coach for 5 years. I saw so many people who were at their worst emotionally, but with a little extra help, they solved their own problems and transformed their relationship to co-parent.

Rather than focusing on feelings and behavior, focus on perceptions

Feelings and behaviors are side effects. They are by-products of perceptions. If you focus only on feelings and behaviors, you have to guess at the reasons why other people are feeling and acting the way they are. More times than not, you will assume incorrectly and respond to them inappropriately. To truly understand someone, you need to understand how they see it.

Silence is golden

Silence has a tendency to make people uncomfortable. Be able to look at the other party and handle the tension silence can cause. Some will say anything to break the tension of silence. Rather than react poorly, do or say nothing, especially if the other party is getting positional or argumentative. Silence has a tendency to make the other party a little uncomfortable and shifts the responsibility for keeping the conversation going to them.

Remain optimistic

No matter what happens, communicate your optimism. Make comments such as, "Well, we both seem to have some strong feelings, but if we keep at it, I'm sure we can work something out," or "I can understand that you feel frustrated; I do as well. Let's review our needs and see what we have in common." Don't give up; you never know when something positive will happen.

Future versus past orientation

When emotions run high, we have a tendency to look to the past to either justify our position or to point out the inadequacy of the other party. This neither helps to form an agreement nor to preserve the relationship. At times it may be helpful to cite examples from the past, but dwelling on history will just escalate the other party's emotions. We can argue what has happened in the past and who has done what to whom, or we can problem-solve about how we want to be different in the future. More times than not, it makes no difference if the alligator came in the front or back door, we need to work on alligator removal.

Turn negative statements into needs

Never defend yourself against negative statements. Instead, simply reflect them back in terms of how you perceive the other party's needs. When you turn negative statements into needs, the other party feels acknowledged, If the other party says, "Here we go again, another worthless meeting. We meet to death around here." Respond with, "I think we all need to have our discussions as productive as possible." Do not say, "I do the best I can; besides, we are more productive than other departments." (Fisher & Ury 1991)

When confronting, start with "I" or "We" messages

When we think of confrontation, we think of telling others off or letting them know that their behavior impacts us in some negative way. Typically we start the confrontation with a *You* message. A *You* message used at the beginning of the confrontation only makes the other party more defensive and emotional. In order to assertively communicate your needs, state them in terms of I messages. While the other party may still get defensive or emotional, the intensity will not be as great.

When being confronted, start with *You* messages to get past the feelings and into the other's perceptions

When confronted, you need to fight the natural tendency to blame, defend, rationalize, minimize or explain. Your first step needs to be one of discovery. You need to find out why they are confronting you. And you need to eliminate the associated feelings of anger and defensiveness. If someone angrily confronts you, reflect it back with a *You* message. This will help you find out why they are angry so you can begin to remove the anger.

If a peer at work were to say sarcastically, "Thanks for nothing." Try responding, "You seem to feel that I've let you down?" Then they will tell you why they are upset with you. You can do something about the problem if you know where they are coming from. Once you find out why they are angry, you have multiple options to problem-solve.

Ask open-ended questions

In any problem-solving event, dialog among parties is important for many reasons. It allows venting, expression of needs, creatively developing solutions and the ability to listen and be heard while enhancing relationships. We need to ask questions that encourage or promote this type of dialog.

Phrase questions to begin with "what, when, where or how" to encourage dialog. Do not ask questions that can be answered with a "yes" or "no." Avoid asking questions that begin with "why." "Why" questions tend to get positional answers.

If the other party appears to be inconsistent or trying to deceive you, use the "detective" method

Only as a last resort should you accuse another party of trying to deceive you. If you are not sure, it's best to first try an indirect method to probe for information. The detective, sensing something was amiss in the witness' statement, would start out with questions like, "Could you help me understand …" or "Maybe I'm missing something here; could you explain how … ." The other party always offers more information to a nonthreatening question.

Confrontation is the best way to nurture an ongoing relationship

Using positive confrontation, we confront perceptions, not feelings and behavior. By doing so, we do not allow other people's feelings and behavior to adversely affect us. If we care enough about others, we need to be able to tell them how they impact us and others around them. If we don't tell them, we enable them to continue to behave in ways that may not be in their best interests. If done appropriately, confrontation strengthens relationships.

Accept responsibility for your own feelings and behavior

Most people are guilty of saying, "You make me so angry," "You are driving me crazy," or "You make me feel worthless." Remember what Eleanor Roosevelt said: "No one can make you feel inferior without your permission." Keep in mind that no one can make you do or feel anything you don't choose to do. You control your own feelings and behavior. Once you accept that you are in control, you are empowered to feel and behave as you deem appropriate — not simply in reaction to others.

If you blow it, accept responsibility and apologize

Apologizing is not an admission of guilt, but simply a statement that you own your responsibility for your behavior. Sometimes apologizing can help set the tone of the discussion so all concerned begin to examine their own feelings and behavior. Instead of blaming our behavior on others or rationalizing, defending or explaining ourselves, we also have the option to "own" our mistake, to say we're sorry and move on.

Rather than saying, "There's a good explanation for why I did it," or "That's not half as bad as what you do," or, "Well, the reason that happened was ..." or "If you would just listen to me, I wouldn't have to yell." Try saying, "I'm sorry I yelled. I guess I really felt the need to be heard, but I went about it in the wrong way." Apologizing is not for the weak. It takes strength to admit you are wrong and move on. But it can work wonders.

Pay attention to nonverbal communication

Ask for clarification if needed. Look for obvious nonverbal communication: scowling and crossing arms, not making eye contact, loud sighs, looking at watch or clock, shaking head "no" or silence. If you see any of these repeatedly, you should comment on the behaviors. But ask for clarification rather than accusing. Don't say, "You're mad and not listening!" Instead, say something like, "It seems as though you are frustrated right now." Even if the person denies there is a problem, they will know that you are picking up on their frustration. Or maybe they haven't realized or admitted they really are angry.

Don't get snagged by barbed wire

Emotions can run high; when they do, be careful not to get snagged by barbed words or phrases such as, "You are never available," "You don't care at all," "All you care about is your department," "You always side with administration," "That's simply not fair!"

Don't react, explain or defend yourself. Try to draw them to your side with statements such as, "It's important to you that I'm available," "Maybe we need to look at ways I can show you that I do see the big picture," "While it may seem to you that I always go along with administration, we just want to find a solution we all can live with." This is difficult to do, but you need to resist being snagged.

Positional power

When people have positional power over you, it means that they have power, a title or line authority that you don't have. You probably cannot force them to do what you want them to do. You may have only limited impact. The power you may have lies in persuasion. Again, if you influence perceptions, you can focus on how to make things better and preserve the relationship.

Remember: If someone attacks, let the person vent and then jump in. Bring him up to your level, but do not descend to his; that is, don't play his game. If you fight back, you take the focus off of the issues. Pick the mountain you want to die on, as I said before. When is it worth fighting, and when is it better to give in?

How important is it?

Ask yourself this question. If you answer it honestly, 8 times out of 10 you'll conclude it isn't that important. One colleague told me, "Pick the mountain you want to die on," meaning that every hill (issue) is not worth fighting over. Decide what is important and what is not. If it's not important, let it go. You'll live longer. Sometimes we over pay emotionally, seeing events as more important than they are. Assign a value to the problem. Is it a 10 cent or a dollar problem, and then give it the appropriate amount of attention.

Don't be the tail on the kite.

If you work or live with someone who is on that

emotional roller coaster (way up and way down), you get the chance to go on the ride for free. But going on the ride is a choice. If you are always reacting to others, you become the tail on the kite: going where the kite goes.

—CHAPTER THREE—

Problem Solving:
Mediation

CHAPTER THREE
Problem Solving: Mediation

There are many ways to solve conflicts. We can smooth others, telling them what they want to hear, or gloss over the issues. Smoothing can be good if someone is angry or there is a mob waiting for you in your office. We can withdraw by choosing not to deal with conflicts. General Custer would have lived longer if he had withdrawn or used retreat. Withdrawal is useful if you are getting angry or the issue is just not worth it. We can make others do what we want by using the forcing—"because I said so." Forcing may be appropriate in an emergency or when legal or ethical issues are involved. We can compromise, in which everyone gives up something to get part of what they wanted.

Using problem-solving techniques is another alternative in dealing with conflict. But it is the one alternative we have the least productive experience with. When problem-solving, we start by simply listening and acknowledging the other person's feelings or thoughts. We can use constructive confrontation to make our points while attempting to preserve the relationship. But about half the time, this alone may be insufficient to really resolve the conflict.

When conflict persists, most of us look outside ourselves for someone to make the decision for us, or we represent our position to some higher authority.

This higher authority could be a court of law, a supervisor, grievance committee, parent, friend, union steward, spouse, consultant or arbitrator. Some groups may simply take a vote. I remind my clients to be careful what they ask for, because they just might get it! Do you really want someone else to decide for you?

If someone decides for us, it may turn into a big win or a big lose proposition. We may or may not get what we want. If the relationship with the other party is ongoing, we risk a win that will damage the relationship. If we win at the expense of the relationship, our win/lose proposition quickly becomes lose/lose. While this may be necessary at times, this approach is more of a last resort. Before getting to that last resort, many companies and individuals are turning to mediation and mediation techniques to resolve their problems.

Mediation is defined as the intervention of a neutral third party in a dispute in an attempt to reconcile differences, usually at the request of all parties.

Mediation is not necessarily a new concept. The roots of mediation can be traced back to international disputes in the 19th century — between Greece and Turkey in 1868-69, between Bolivia and Chile in 1882, and Germany and Spain in 1885. Mediation was advocated and promoted at the Hague conferences of 1885 and 1907. Later the League of Nations provided for mediation of disputes culminating in the United Nations procedures for obligatory mediation for member nations. Closer to home the United States formed the Federal Mediation and Conciliation Service in 1947. This agency offers mediation services in handling disputes between labor and management, or it can enter into the negotiation process when interstate commerce is affected.

Benefits of mediation include:

• Empowerment

• Orientation toward the future

• Win/win mutual agreement

• Enhanced relationships

• Cost effectiveness

• Informal atmosphere

• Confidentiality

• Participatory process

Take, for example, divorce and custody mediation. In days gone by, divorcing couples would hire two attorneys and battle in court over such issues as who would get what possessions, who would get custody of the children, and when would each parent be with the children. Frequently, divorcing couples would not speak to each other directly, but only through their attorneys. The conventional wisdom was that two people mired in this type of conflict could not possibly come together to make rational decisions about their children's future. Someone had to do it for them. (A poor assumption, and a costly one!) Typically, one parent would win big and the other lose big. And in the final analysis, every family member came out a loser.

Nothing is further from the truth than to think two people can't handle their own conflict. In fact, national statistics indicate that in divorce and custody mediation, mutual agreements are reached with divorcing couples 60 percent to 70 percent of the time. Now, some will say that is a low number, but litigation rarely produces an agreement that is truly in the best interest of the children.

For almost 20 years I was a court-approved divorce mediator. Couples were referred by the court when they could not agree on shared parenting time or matters of custody. These were angry (scared and hurt) people (who wouldn't spit on each other if they were on fire), and I had three hours to help them decide how to raise their kids for the rest of their lives.

Research indicates that mediated agreements have a lower incidence of later winding up in court as opposed to judge-decreed agreements. Also, ongoing relationships, as fragile as they may be, are better preserved, laying a positive foundation for future problem-solving and conflict resolution. Mediation gives us a structure to challenge old perceptions, to involve those affected by the outcomes, to create ownership of problems and solutions, and to promote win/win agreements in a non-adversarial, partnership atmosphere.

Mediation techniques can be applied as a whole process, or they can be used in segments that will be helpful in your day-to-day interactions with others as you go about transforming your work or family relationships. In a company, the result will be good working relationships that promote quality services and products. In a family, the result can be healthy family interactions, regardless of the family structure.

The Customary Problem Solving Approach

The best way to illustrate the basic principles of mediation is to contrast them with the way most groups, companies and families approach problem solving. As you read through, please note the difference between **positional** and **needs-based** problem solving. The customary three-step problem-solving approach is also called **positional bargaining** or **positional problem solving**.

It can be diagrammed as follows:

1. Identify issues or problems.

2. Formulate positions or solutions.

3. Discuss.

Step #1: Identify Issues or Problems

While this step is essentially the same in both problem-solving methods, a common mistake is to spend too little time concretely identifying all the issues. If the issues are ill-defined, there likely will be little agreement that the issues identified are the major ones, and it won't make any difference what solutions are developed. If a physician misdiagnoses a patient's condition, it won't matter what new drug or high-tech treatment is prescribed; it won't treat the pathology. So it's always important that the issues be operationally defined and the participants be able to buy in to them.

Step #2: Positions/Solutions

Once the issues are identified — or sometimes even before the issues are identified — we usually start formulating positions or solutions. Perhaps, we even start to muster support among our peers and others for our positions, like picking sides on the playground. We begin politicking to see who is for us or against us. We may start calling in our markers, favors owed us from others.

In a fast-paced, ever-changing environment, once a problem surfaces, people immediately start asking the question, "What are we going to do about it?" This is when factionalism or sub-grouping occurs. Now that all parties have formulated their positions, the next step is to convene some type of forum to select the best position.

Step #3: Discussion

Now a meeting is held to discuss the different positions. In reality, what happens is that we simply argue over who has the better position. Each side is trying to win, consciously or unconsciously, at the expense of the other. This is the methodology most of us grew up with.

No one is listening to understand the other side's position, but only listening for ways to counter. This funnel-down technique is commonly used, and it commonly results in an either/or proposition that promotes winners and losers. When one side wins, it damages the quality of the ongoing relationships. Rarely does the position with the best merit win. The winner is the side which makes the most persuasive argument. Often no agreement is reached, and all parties suffer the consequences (hurt feelings, resentment, strained relationships, lower- quality products or services ... sometimes even war).

This positional method is how families solve problems most of the time. Let's take, for example, the husband and wife trying to decide what to do on Friday night (the issue). The wife declares that she would like to go out for dinner, and the husband counters with his desire to go to the movies (their positions). Having committed to their positions early in the problem-solving process, they decide to sit down and talk about it (the discussion). The ensuing discussion usually sounds something like this:

Husband: "I want to go to a movie."

Wife: "I want to go out for dinner."

Husband: "Well, hon, we could eat popcorn at the theater. They have that new popcorn oil that's non-caloric."

Wife: "That's ridiculous. Besides, I just want to spend some time with you."

Husband: "We could get two seats right next to each other."

Wife: "You're not listening to me. We can never seem to talk."

Husband: "We have 15 minutes to kill to and from the theater. We can chat our fool heads off."

Wife: (angry and frustrated) "Fine! We'll just go to the lousy movie. We always do what you want to anyway;" or, "Just forget it. It isn't worth all this. I don't want to do anything now. I'm staying home."

Husband: (angry and frustrated) "We do not do

everything I want to do. Just last week we went to your sister's when I didn't want to. Sometimes you can be such a martyr!" or, "Fine! We'll just stay home then."

Oh boy, sounds like another fun time on Friday night, doesn't it? In some relationships, this is all too typical. Each spouse commits too early in the problem-solving process to a position. While the wife tries to give reasons why they should go out for dinner, the husband counters her reasons to fit his position. The wife begins to get frustrated and starts blaming, and the husband gets defensive and lashes back.

Another example: Let's say the boss, Ms. Fields, is having a discussion with one of her employees, Mr. Jones. She feels that expenses can be reduced best by eliminating positions. Mr. Jones wants to try to forestall that by cutting equipment and expenses first:

Ms. Fields: "Did you consider my cost savings proposal, Mr. Jones?"

Mr. Jones: "Yes, and I was wondering if we could take a look at different alternatives to layoffs."

Ms. Fields: "These aren't layoffs, they're position eliminations!"

Mr. Jones: "Fine, but can't we hold off on ordering the new equipment until sales catch up?"

Ms. Fields: "That won't work. We need the equipment to produce the products to make sales."

Mr. Jones: "What's the use if we don't have anyone to operate the equipment?"

Ms. Fields: "This isn't the time to be difficult, Mr.

Jones. The expenses are on the salary side, not the supply or equipment side. I can't believe you don't see that. Maybe you're too soft. Know this: If we don't cut salaries, we'll close our doors!"

Mr. Jones: "I guess there's no choice then." (Thinking, "Why did she ask me if she already had her mind made up?") (Mastroianni 2003)

In this customary three-step approach to problem-solving, we formulate positions. In the alternative approach of mediation, we formulate needs instead of positions. This is referred to as needs-based bargaining or needs-based problem-solving. It can be diagrammed as follows:

1. Identify issue/problem

2. Discussion
   • Needs
   • Shared interests
   • Objective criteria

3. Position/solution

Step #1: Identify Issues or Problems

If you are a participant, let the other party go first. Parents may want to let the children speak first. This may be something new in your family, but it shows that you respect them. If you do this, they are more likely to listen to you after you have listened to them first. The following principles will help to facilitate mutual identification of, and agreement on, the issues.

Venting/story-telling: Each party needs to be able to vent uninterrupted, getting their thoughts and feelings off their chests in front of all the parties involved. In essence, they need to tell their stories. Telling their stories has a cathartic effect, in that people usually feel better after they have vented in a safe environment. All parties, having heard the honest thoughts and feelings of others, can begin to appreciate how others perceive the issues and how the issues impact them. The party telling her story also can hear and evaluate, maybe for the first time, her own thoughts and perceptions.

Reflective listening: Reflective listening can help you encourage the story-telling and communicate your understanding of the issues. If the party telling their story is talkative, **passive listening** works well. As someone is talking, a few "Uh-huhs" or eye contact with a few head nods will accomplish the task. If the other party is not particularly talkative, eye contact and **silence** can be used to encourage them to communicate. As you listen for the issues, reflect back on what you hear with statements such as "Sounds like that's important to you," "Seems that how we communicate is a big issue for you," or "When I don't talk to you first, you feel I'm going behind your back?"

Issue identification: As each party tells their story, listen carefully for what seem to be major points or issues. Sometimes participants will bring concrete issues to the table. If this is the case, issue identification is a matter of understanding participants' issues, helping to ensure that their issues are reflective of the situation. Narrow the focus so that each issue is defined well enough to be workable. Sometimes parties will bring feelings to the table. Feelings may be generalized, with attitudes such as, "This family sucks," or "This department is a mess." Rather than attend to the feelings, attempt to remove them and help the party clarify the issues. Reflective listening and open-ended questions can be used to do this. Ask questions such as, "Sounds like you feel very strongly about the family's situation; what exactly do you feel sucks?" Or, "I can understand that you feel the department is in chaos, but what is it that you see?" The task at hand is to help all parties define their issues.

As you ask open-ended questions, reflect feelings and help narrow down the issues. Paraphrasing each party's issues will help to clarify the issues and create buy-in for all. Make comments such as, "Your unhappiness with the family appears to be caused by us (parents) always telling you what to do." Or, "Seems to me — based on what you're saying — that the chaos in the department is due, in part, to a lack of face-to-face communication." The party will either agree or disagree. If the party responds with, "Yeah, that's right. Bingo. Exactly," then the issue has been correctly identified. If not, continue to paraphrase or ask questions that require the party to zero in on the issue.

Issue consensus: Always listen for any areas of agreement as the issues are clarified. Listen for common issues and comment on them. For example, if you hear all parties identifying that how they talk to each other is a common issue, you can say, "Sounds like how you treat each other verbally is an issue for everybody in the department, including management." As a participant, listen to the other parties' issues, notice how close they might be to yours and comment on them. Chances are they are roughly the same. For example, in the family, if the kids' issue is that you yell too much and you think the kids are disrespectful at times, try a comment like, "Seems like one of the issues we share is how we all talk to each other."

Always listen for issues common to all and get consensus. Most parties involved in dispute resolution will try to sharpen their differences, initially. After all, it is the differences that have caused the difficulties. But this sets a negative tone to the mediation and can block the entire process of getting agreements. Momentum is important in dispute resolution, especially when issues are numerous. It doesn't make any sense to initially emphasize how far apart parties are. Instead, start with how close they are or what they seem to have in common. This, then, can set a positive tone and help participants see that their issues actually are solvable.

As you clarify and reach consensus on the major issues, you are creating an allegiance with the parties involved. This is another form of "transitioning," in which we begin to transition away from a position where we see each other as the problem to a position where we see the issues as the problem. Therefore, the parties are coming together to deal with a common enemy (issues). Ury (1992) in his book, *Getting Past No*, calls this the side-by- side strategy of negotiation. Rather than face-off against another party, you invite them to your side to help deal with the common problems. Work groups consisting of employees and management transition away from blaming each other to rallying together to tackle their problems. Family members transition away from perceiving each other as uncaring or hostile and focus their collective energies on how to deal differently with their common problems.

Every now and then a party will have an issue that others do not share, or more likely, do not see as important. These issues can't be ignored. Never argue over whether a concern is an issue or not, nor its relative importance. In an ongoing relationship, if one party has an issue, it is an issue to all and must be respected as such by all.

As in the customary three-step positional problem solving approach, all the issues in conflict need to be identified and operationally defined with buy-in from all parties. This is where reflective listening is an invaluable tool to generate comments such as, "Sounds like we all need more communication internally to be on the cutting edge." Or, "Seems most of us think that all the yelling and screaming is not getting us anywhere."

It doesn't make any sense to argue over whether or not something is an issue. If one party in an ongoing relationship perceives something as an important issue, it is.

Once the issues are defined and some type of consensus is reached, it's time to move on to the second step. Herein lies the difference in the two approaches.

Step #2: Discussion

In the mediation approach, you simply invert steps 2 and 3, where the discussion occurs before positions are formulated and the politicking begins. The discussion focuses on **needs, shared interests** and **objective criteria** rather than positions or solutions (Fisher & Ury, 1991).

Rather than asking, "What should we do?" a needs-based problem solver asks, "What does everyone need?" (needs). While needs may vary, they can often be categorized into the basic needs that most people, organizations or corporations have in common: truth, communication, honesty and respect.

Rather than initially focusing on our differences, let's focus on things we have in common (shared interests). In divorce and custody mediation, the mediator will focus on the love and concern parents share for their children, how both are important to the children's growth and development in spite of their differences. At work, we can use mediation techniques with a peer by starting with the interests we share. For example, we both want an equitable work load, to get off work on time, to have cooperative and collaborative relationships, to have a non-hostile work environment and respect for diversity. Initially, we can sharpen our shared interests, not our differences.

Once issues have been identified and consensus established, the groundwork needs to be laid for getting agreements. To do so, the issues must be further defined or **reframed** into needs. This transforms the negotiations into a needs-based negotiation. In my experience, I've found that most issues can be reframed into the following needs:

Empowerment/respect: With this need, parties often feel that their thoughts or needs don't matter. Most people need some input or control regarding their lives or work. They need to feel valued and empowered to give input and make some decisions. When agreements pay attention to empowerment/respect needs, all parties become stakeholders; they have ownership, and the likelihood of compliance with the agreements improves.

Trust: Parties at times may feel they cannot believe one or all of the others involved. In an ongoing relationship all parties have trust needs, whether they are parent-child, peer-peer, management-employee or nation-nation. If trust is a need, a good agreement will reflect this need in detailing how this need will be met.

Communication: Parties often feel that how they communicate is not productive — that it is inflammatory, adversarial or nonexistent. In business or families, Codes of Conduct can be established. How parties communicate is just as important, if not more important, than the agreements reached. If the parties can communicate effectively, almost any issue can be worked out.

Truth/honesty: Parties sometimes feel they were lied to — or more commonly, have misperceived another party's statements or actions. Needs that focus on truth and honesty are sometimes cleared up in the mediation process as all parties tell their stories, identify their issues and look at their needs.

Negative assumptions and misperceptions can be exposed and explained. In any case, the need for truth and honesty should be addressed for any agreement to be long-lasting.

Turn negative statements into need based statements: Negotiations can break down or turn hostile when parties begin making negative statements to each other. Sometimes negative words, barbs, digs or attacking statements will elicit equally negative statements, or worse, from others. It is the skillful mediator, participant, parent or coach who can take that negative statement and turn it into a needs-based statement.

Just as I discussed in the chapter on positive and effective communication, rather than attack in retaliation or refuse to participate, we need to throw out, or jujitsu, the emotion and identify the need embedded in the emotion. For example, if a person were to say, "Well you are such a back- stabber and gossip. At least I don't do that!" we shouldn't respond with a negative comment about her. Instead ask, "To work better together, you need for me to be honest and tell you and not others what I think?" After that party agrees, you then can identify a need such as, "I can try coming to you first with a problem, but I need to feel you are willing to listen and not get angry." You might respond to the same statement with, "Seems that honesty (removing the words back-stabber and gossip) is a big need for you. How do others feel about honesty in this department?"

Just about any negative statement can be turned into a needs-based statement:

Family

• I'm sick of Jennifer always getting her way (you need to be treated equally).

• I have to do all the work around here (you need a fair work schedule).

• No one listens to what I say (you need to be heard and acknowledged).

Business

• That department never helps us out during peak times (you need everyone to pitch in).

• We're sick of the gossip that's spread around here (you need people to refrain from

  spreading rumors).

• I feel like I'm taking orders from peers, and I don't have a say (you need some control).

Agreeing on objective criteria is another mediation technique. If necessary, we can look to some measurement, benchmark or expert to help in the process (to establish objective criteria). Using the Blue Book value is helpful in buying a used car. In divorce or custody mediation, sometimes counselors are called in for their opinions on what would be appropriate, given a child's age or maturity. Or accountants may be asked to render an opinion on the equitable division of assets. In business, consultants are asked to make recommendations on specific problems.

Step #3: Positions/Solutions

At this point, the group needs to consider the expressed needs, shared interests or objective criteria from previous discussions to begin generating solutions or positions to meet everyone's needs and the shared interests. The question becomes, "What can we agree on that satisfies our needs and shared interests?" More times than not positions and solutions will emerge that no one thought of at the beginning. This is the creative funneling-up process at work. Here we are expanding the pie rather than dividing it (Ury, 1991).

Committing to a position too early in the problem-solving process blocks creativity and doesn't take into account the other party's needs and shared interests. Why just have two ways (yours and theirs) when numerous solutions can be developed that meet specific needs? More importantly, a win/win agreement can be reached to meet the needs of all concerned while preserving relationships.

Back to the husband and wife. Had their problem-solving discussion been needs-based, it would have sounded like this:

Wife: "Tonight I need to get out of the house and just relax a little, away from the kids."

Husband: "I don't want to get all dressed up or be around a lot of people. I've been teaching all day and want to relax too."

Wife: "I don't want to be around a bunch of people, either. But I am getting a little hungry."

Husband: "Well, I'm not that hungry. Besides, if I eat one more burger or pizza this week, I'll explode."

Wife: "Maybe we could just go for a drive or go to the park for awhile."

Husband: "A drive sounds good. It gets us out of

the house without bumping into a lot of people, and if we decide later to get something to eat, there are plenty of fast food restaurants on the west side of town."

This sounds just a little different than the positional problem-solving approach, and it produces a different outcome. Here the husband and wife first discuss needs and look for shared interests rather than staking out a position. Subsequently, once the identified positions or solutions are developed—that neither thought of initially—they find the solution meets their mutual needs. This solution never would have been generated by the customary, positional method, because the spouses were locked into their respective positions of dinner or a movie.

Revisiting our cost-cutting scenario from the mediation (needs-based) approach may sound like this:

Ms. Fields: "I need to make sure we reduce expenses, and the salary budget is where we need to look."

Mr. Jones: "I need to work with you on expense reduction too, but I'd like to do so without putting our people out of work."

Ms. Fields: "Maybe we can talk to them and get them to agree to a wage freeze instead of job elimination."

Mr. Jones: "Maybe we can have enough people leaving through early retirement or by not filling open positions that costs are saved without laying off."

Ms. Fields: "Work up the numbers, and let's see what we have." (Mastroianni 2003)

Again, once the needs were generated, positions emerged (wage freeze, early retirement, vacant positions left open) that no one thought of at the beginning. The mediation approach can be used in interpersonal relationships at home and at work.

Norm's Nuggets

These "nuggets" are therapy techniques, analogies, metaphors, sayings, quotes from others, common sense pieces, problem solving and communication tips that I have found helpful in my work. I would like to share them with you. In this chapter I have included the following nuggets:

NORM'S NUGGETS

Problem Solving Nuggets: Tips

Rather than dealing with positions, look for the needs that the position is meeting

Don't immediately counter or react negatively to the other's position. Wait. Remember positions are end products. They are the things that the other party feels will meet their needs. Once you can identify the other party's needs, then you can create multiple positions that meet those needs and yours.

If the other party commits too early in the problem solving process, help them back down with dignity

Since most people are not familiar with problem-solving techniques, they may make the error of committing too early in the process. Some think that playing hardball is a positive strategy, and they tell you that this is their final proposal and may threaten some consequence if you don't take it.

When this happens, do not react to their position, but allow them room to back down with dignity. This helps preserve the relationship. If the union negotiator says, "This is our final offer—take it or we'll strike," you say, "I'm sure that's one option, but let's see if there might be another way to avoid that option and meet your needs." (Ury 1993)

Funnel up, not down

Most businesses try to problem-solve by reducing their options to two and picking one over the other. This creates winners and losers and damages the quality of the relationships. Why would you want only a couple of possible solutions to a problem? Creating multiple options to solve problems (funneling up) is the best way to go. Do not "boil it down to two and pick" or employ either/or thinking. When we create multiple options, we can find new solutions—usually ones that no one thought of initially—that meet most of the parties' needs.

Begin with a common ground, not differences

It is natural to start with our differences, because our differences cause our problems. Rather, look for common ground and say "yes" as many times as possible as well as asking questions that elicit yes from the other party. Use statements such as, "I'm glad we could both agree to mediate," "Seems like we all want to solve our differences in different ways," or "Yes, you have a point." Reflecting back what someone just said will elicit a "Yes, that's right" response.

Be open to persuasion

Don't go into any meeting or enter into any problem-solving event without the ability to learn from the others involved. A closed mind or righteous attitude will doom any negotiations. In any interaction, be receptive to the other party's views and be willing to be persuaded. Being willing to be persuaded can be contagious. When you demonstrate your open-mindedness, others will likely follow. Sometimes it is better to open your mind and shut your mouth!

As Gandhi said, "An eye for an eye and everyone goes blind."

Don't lower yourself to the other party's tactics if they become demeaning. Continue trying to develop mutually beneficial solutions. Fisher and Brown (1992) in their book, *Getting Together*, describe an unconditionally constructive strategy as "doing only those things that are both good for the relationship and good for us, whether they reciprocate or not." For example, ask for the other party's input even if they don't ask you. If they are acting emotionally, you try to balance emotions with reason. If they misunderstand you, try to understand them. Even if they are not listening, consult them before deciding on matters that affect them.

Mirror their style

It is important to show respect in any problem-solving situation. If there are different cultures, cultural styles also need to be respected. One way to show respect and thus nonverbally communicate respect for the other party is to accommodate or mirror their style. If they speak slowly, do the same. If they are formal, be formal. If they take time to pause and reflect, you do likewise. This is called pacing, and it helps people feel empathy with you and your needs.

The process is equally important, if not more so, than the outcome

What we decide to do differently may or may not be effective, but if we negotiate based on needs or shared interests, we can always come back to the table because the relationship is preserved. Preserving the relationship is a primary goal, as well as reaching an agreement.

Start with the easiest thing first

If there are multiple issues or problems to deal with, go with the smallest, easiest issue. Start with the least important issue in order to build some positive momentum before tackling harder issues. We have a tendency to want to start with the most glaring or emotionally charged issue. Resist this tendency, as it can put an initially negative spin on the whole problem-solving process.

Always leave the door open

If the problem solving or negotiation is getting stuck or you are starting to lose it, don't say, "This is getting us nowhere. I don't think this is solvable." Rather, say, "Well, I'd hoped we could have worked this out. We still have two days before the deadline. I would be receptive to another meeting. Please give me a call." The majority of agreements are reached in the 11th hour. If you shut the door because you get angry, you could blow an opportunity to reach an agreement.

Don't threaten, but warn of natural consequences

A threat is a promise of negative consequences

usually imposed by you. A warning is a glimpse into the future of what may happen. At work, save your threats to go to the boss as a last resort. Instead try to explain the potential impact on the company if things do not get done: "We need to get the diversity training implemented as soon as possible, because we don't want the employees feeling like we don't care!" (Ury 1993)

Consider objective criteria

Another strategy in problem solving is to look to various sources for information or ideas. Sometimes this is a neutral strategy in that we are not picking one party's idea over another. We're agreeing to find a third party to help. Suggesting that an expert opinion be sought is one way to offer a neutral strategy. Benchmarking with other companies or groups is another neutral strategy if problem solving bogs down. If you differ with your real estate agent over the asking price for your home, you may think you only have three options: You can stick with your asking price, accept the realtor's price or split the difference. However, with these choices, it won't be possible for both parties to feel their needs are getting met. Either just one party got their way or both got only part of what they thought was fair. If both parties could agree to get two appraisals and take the average, everyone wins. No one loses or feels cheated. (Fisher/Ury 1991)

Offer choices, rather than asking for acceptance or rejection of your proposal

Try to avoid saying, "Take it or leave it," "Should

we or shouldn't we," or "Can I or can't I." This forces
the other party into an either/or proposition. It is
better for all concerned to be able to select from
multiple options to meet the needs of all parties. It
is the shrewd 16-year-old who, rather than ask mom
if he can use the car to go to the movies, says, "Mom,
I want to use the car to go to the show. Would it be
more convenient for you if I went to the 6 o'clock or
8 o'clock showing?" Never ask a yes or no question if
you don't want a no answer. (Mastroianni 2003)

Invite criticism

Most people do not like criticism. But, in problem
solving you need to invite it. Criticism gives you clues
about the needs of the other party. Don't be afraid to
ask the other party, "What is it about this solution
that doesn't seem to meet your needs?" Inviting
criticism also allows the other party to vent their
frustration, which in turn should make them easier
to deal with.

Don't commit too soon in the problem solving process.

Even if you are sure that your position is the only
position that is workable, don't propose it or bring
it up until the end, or near the end, of the problem-
solving process. Keep an open mind as you listen to
the other side. Enter any problem-solving activity
with the ability to be persuaded. If you commit too
early to a position, it forces the other party into an
either/or (your way or no way) proposition and halts
the process.

Collect "yes's"

In his book *Getting Past No*, William Ury suggests that if you're trying to help parties in problem solving, comment on areas of possible agreement. Comments such as, "Seems like these issues are very important to everyone concerned," "While we might not agree on the cause of the problems, sounds like you agree on the adverse effects the problems are causing," "Both of you are after a fair and equitable settlement," or "It would appear that we all think raises are a good idea; we just need to determine how much." This helps set a positive tone for the process and demonstrates that the parties are not as far apart as they think. (Ury 1993)

Grab agreements

As agreements are reached, grab them. As soon as the parties say, "I could live with that," "That idea would meet my needs and deal with the issues," or, "We could try that," grab that agreement and move on to the next issue or end the mediation. To do so, either as a participant or mediator, you simply restate the agreement and ask if your interpretation is correct. If so, then it needs to be documented, in writing, on the spot, to be included in a memorandum of agreement or written action plan.

Don't belabor the agreement or play devil's advocate by asking "What if ..." questions. Just get the agreement down and move on.

—CHAPTER FOUR—

Being Better with Ourselves and Others

CHAPTER FOUR

Being Better with Ourselves and Others

As I said in the introduction I have found that most people, to be the best they can be with themselves and others, need three things:

First, we need a way to understand ourselves and others.

Human Behavior: Cognitive Based Model
Second, we need to communicate and listen better.

Positive and Effective Communication Thirdly, we need different ways to solve problems that enhances our relationships.

Problem Solving: Mediation

Now in this chapter you can apply all the above to ourselves and our most important relationships with others. First, to love ourselves (OK, maybe *like* ourselves) and second, to have the healthiest relationships at home, and at work, as possible. I offer the following nuggets:

Norm's Nuggets

These "nuggets" are therapy techniques, analogies, metaphors, sayings, quotes from others, common sense pieces, problem solving and communication tips that I have found helpful in my work. I would like to share them with you. In this chapter I have included the following nuggets:

NORM'S NUGGETS

Self-Esteem and Relationships

Self Esteem

If you *do* what you have always *done*, you will *get* what you always *got*.

Not sure who said this, but it sounds better than the definition of "insanity is doing the same thing over and over again, expecting a different result." See, it has nothing to do with sanity and seems to resonate better.

Do you hear yourself?

Most people these days talk so fast I'm not so sure they hear what they are saying or how they are saying it. Especially if they are talking positively (not bragging or boasting) about themselves or reframing their old perceptions. So, I will stop them and say, "Did you just hear yourself?" and watch for them to take a breath and smile. Now they heard themselves!

Don't "should" on yourself or engage in "Musturbation."

Albert Ellis in his landmark book, *Guide to*

Rational Living talked about should, must, ought to, have to — and how these statements set us up to fail. Have-to, ought-to, must and should are labels we use in an attempt to motivate ourselves — for example: "I have to do well;" "I must succeed;" "I should do more." When we label events in this fashion we become apathetic, unmotivated and setup for failure. Moreover, when we apply labels to others, such as, "He shouldn't treat me like that," or, "I have to be treated with respect," we become resentful that others can't reach our level of expectations. These statements produce unnecessary pressure and resentment. It doesn't matter if something should have happened or not, it did — and we need to deal with it. So I suggest we don't "should" on ourselves or get caught up in mustrubation.

Either you manage it or it manages you.

All of us have something we have to deal with that is not going away. Whether that's a physical issue, addiction, life experience, family dysfunction, a medical condition or whatever. There is no getting around, over or under it. If you can't cure it, you need to manage it. Or, it manages you. You may not control something happening, but you can control the impact it has on you. Is it devastating or annoying? Don't give it any more power than it already has.

The brain processes pain in chunks.

When something traumatic happens, the brain needs time to process it. It is like the old saying, "The best way to eat the elephant is one bite at a time … you can't swallow it whole." Talking it out, writing it out and/or engaging in bilateral exercise (running, swimming, drumming) will help the brain process the pain. The brain is trying to make sense of something that initially doesn't make sense. Intrusive thoughts, moodiness, anger, anxiety, and edginess are all common problems. The brain has a wonderful way to heal itself, if you let it. It will take time and an openness on your part to let it work its way through.

Most clients are just out of balance: work, life, fun.

Think of your life as a pie chart. Work, social life, family and individual time pieces need to add up to 100. When one piece gets too big or too small, we get out of balance. You need to keep an eye on your inner pie chart and re-balance on occasion.

Machine in the basement.

Sometimes, even when we know better, we don't take good care of ourselves or our primary relationships. I like the analogy of the machine in the basement. If you had a machine in the basement that made thousands of dollars, took care of the house, drove the kids to their activities, mowed the lawn, washed the car, did the grocery shopping and visited routinely with your mother in law, you would take very good care of that machine. You would check it daily, polish it, change its oil and make sure it had everything it needed to help your family. Well, you're that machine, and if that machine isn't well maintained, everyone suffers.

Airline Oxygen Masks

Here is another great self-care analogy. When

the flight attendants go over the safety procedures on the airplane, they tell passengers to put on their mask first. Because if you are gasping for breath, it's really tough to help others. This is a good analogy for parents, and especially Moms.

Gas station of life.

One more good self-care (or lack thereof) analogy is where do we go or what do we do to fill up our tank? We all need to stop at the gas station of life and refuel. But most don't do that, and instead run on fumes. If you have a full tank, those around you benefit as well because you are much more pleasant to be around.

"DON'T" on cell phone.

Ever wish you had the strength or better judgment not to answer a call or not to respond impulsively to a text from an ex-relationship-person, especially when you were depressed, lonely or angry? A client replaced the person's name with DON'T. So, when she saw DON'T on the phone, she was able to wait and respond when she wanted to (if at all).

Better hope you are part of the problem.

When things go bad, we have a tendency to look externally or to others to explain the way we feel or to understand what happened. If you are part of the problem, you have the ability to influence the problem. Look at yourself first, to say, "If I change something about myself, would that make a difference?"

"If I don't argue, there's no argument. Takes at least two to have an argument."

"Maybe I could listen more and not try to fix it."

"I could model for my partner how I would like to be treated."

"I can choose not to be codependent or enabling if a loved one has an addiction."

While we may not have much control of external events, we at least have control of the impact these events or people have on us. Eleanor Roosevelt once said, " No one can make you feel inferior without your consent." It takes one to dish it out, but it takes you to accept it. How true!

Batter in a slump.

When an episode of depression, anxiety, self-loathing or just a generalized feeling of being overwhelmed happens, you can't just try harder. If a batter in baseball gets in to a hitting slump, the coach doesn't just say swing harder! No, the batter goes back and revisits the fundamentals: grip … stance … eye on the ball etc. It is the same with us, when we get in a funk; go back to the basics: perception accuracy … self-care … self-talk … control/no control … importance … medication, etc.

Solar system.

This is a great analogy for managing friend and family relationships. Some planets (friends/family) orbit closer to the sun (you) and some further away. At times, some planets need to move out further into space and others need to move in closer, but all stay in the solar system. This moves people away from all or nothing or absolute thinking.

½ a glass of water.

Is it half full or half empty? Reality says it's just

a ½ glass of water. It has no value until you give it value. Me, I'm going to lean in the direction of half full. Which way do you want to make the mistake?

What do you want on your tombstone?

Organizational consultant, Steven Covey once said, "Begin with the end in mind." Sometimes I ask my clients, "What would you want on your tombstone? Pain in the Ass? Perfectionistic? Pretty Negative? Good at Finding the One Thing Wrong? Cranky? Or ... Kind? Loving Spouse? Great Parent?" Perhaps you need to begin with the end in mind. Changing perceptions changes feelings.

If you skin your own skunks, everyone else's don't stink so bad.

The sooner you can be good with yourself, the sooner others don't seem so bad. Taking care of one's own issues first before trying to change others is a good idea, because you have more control over you and less over others. But, when we rationalize that as soon as they change we will be better, this gives away a lot of power to others.

Talk to yourself as you would your best friend.

Sometimes we can be our own worst critics. What's up with that? I hear clients all the time bad mouth themselves and share self-loathing thoughts. I always ask, "What you just said about yourself, would you say the same thing about a friend to that friend?" Of course not! So why say it to yourself? We need to be as supportive to ourselves as we would be to a friend who is struggling.

Can't catch a fish if you don't get your worm wet.

My brother, Steve, used to always say this, and of course you can take it many ways. Given its many interpretations, I like it to mean, "You will never know unless you try." But it does get people's attention.

Sometimes our weaknesses are just our strengths over-used.

Not sure who said this, but it is very true. I see this at home and at work. When we get under pressure, we consciously or unconsciously do what we feel we do best. But sometimes that can be a weakness. There is nothing wrong with being emphatic, but I can be too emphatic and be codependent. I can be assertive, but over use assertiveness, and others will avoid you. Being a hard worker is good unless I try too hard and make things worse. Having many tools in the tool box is a good thing.

Relationships

Make deposits in the relationship.

Stephen Covey, the management consultant, speaks of relationships like bank accounts. This makes some sense. I encourage couples to see their marriage or relationship like a bank account that needs deposits on a regular basis. From time to time there will be withdrawals, and we need to make sure we have enough in the account to cover the withdrawals. This needs to be intentional, just like banking, and not just when we can get around to it. I see a lot of relationships that are bankrupt purely by neglect. Which brings me to the next two concepts:

List of things to do today: Where is the relationship?

Most of us keep a list of things to do. There are even apps for that, that can be updated by Siri®, Alexa®, Google Home®, among others by simply speaking out loud! We delight in crossing off tasks to gain a sense of accomplishment. We manage tasks such as making appointments, paying bills, things to clean, sending cards, groceries, soccer try outs, picking up dry cleaning or refilling a prescription, etc. But where on that list is your relationship? It doesn't even make the list, does it? Why?

Hmmmm....Well, over time with careers, kids, homes, the dog, the relationship slides down the food chain and becomes a second thought. When everything else is taken care of, then we can focus on us. Do you ever totally complete everything on a to do list?

Every healthy relationship I have seen has been the result of a lot of work and a priority. The relationship needs to be like the mortgage, where that bill is a priority at the beginning of each month. Most of us don't just spend our money and hope we have enough left over at the end of the month to cover the mortgage. Making the relationship a priority (maybe in the top 3 on the list of things to do) is a gift to you, your kids and others in your life, as you will be more pleasant to be around.

Commit random acts of kindness.

Just as the relationship needs to be on the list of things to do today, what you do is equally important.

In order to maintain or help a "stalled" relationship, I encourage partners to intentionally commit random acts of kindness. Do something that your partner will appreciate that says you are important to me. As you pull into the driveway or hear the garage door go up what acts of kindness do you plan to commit?

• Pay a verbal compliment.

• Say thank you twice.

• Hold a kiss or a hug a little longer.

• Sit closer together.

• A card under a pillow, in a suitcase, lunch bag or front seat of their car.

• Fold the laundry.

• Put a hand on a shoulder, pat on the back or a tap on the bottom.

• Tell then they are coolest thing since sliced bread.

• Ask about their day.

• Watch a Hallmark movie or football game.

• Make the bed.

• Clean up after yourself.

• Catch them doing something you like and acknowledge it.

Can't justify your bad behavior because your partner does it.

It is very common for couples to argue about who does what to whom. And as a defense, they say, "Well but you do …" or "You do it too!" Two wrongs certainly don't make a right. Each transgression needs to be addressed separately. Just because your partner does something harmful, don't use it as an excuse for your poor behavior.

Problem or not ...?

Too many couples, families, work groups spend too much time arguing about whether something is a problem or not. Well, in an on-going relationship, if one party or group feels something is a problem, it is! Then we can move on to problem solving rather than arguing. If your 5 year old thinks there is a ghost in the closet, you can spend all night explaining that there is no such thing as ghosts, or you can open up the window and shoo the ghost out. Problem solved!

Code of conduct for couples, families and work groups.

Sometimes couples, families and work groups need a procedure for communication and behavior. It can be developed by the employees or families so they can buy into it. It will encourage people to solve problems at the lowest levels possible and increase positive communication. It will be a procedure or contract written by a group for the group called a CODE OF CONDUCT.

Companies and families often have unwritten codes of conduct. In a company, these are often defined by the corporate culture. The more authoritarian the culture, the more the unwritten code of conduct encourages people to keep their mouths shut, not to rock the boat and not to lose their jobs. Here is an unwritten code of conduct:

1) Don't confront anyone.

2) If you do confront, rip the other person to shreds.

3) Don't discuss single issues: Wait and collect them, and cash them in.

4) Make sure you tell others rather than the person involved.

5) Break times, lunch or after work are good times to talk about others behind their backs.

6) Anger and rage are fine ways of expressing yourself.

7) Keep quiet and internalize your frustrations.

8) Be competitive with others and win; let them lose.

9) Be suspicious and mistrusting. Just because you're not paranoid doesn't mean everyone isn't out to get you.

10) Don't share ideas. Nothing ever changes anyway, and you might lose your job.

Similar to the workplace, an unwritten code of conduct exists in our homes. In a family, it may look something like this:

1) When someone is bothering us, make sure we tattle to Mom or Dad.

2) If Dad comes home angry, leave him alone until he is happy again.

3) When angry with each other, we will give each other the silent treatment.

4) The children are great verbal punching bags in case we are having a bad day and need to take our frustrations out on people who won't fight back or threaten us.

5) Choose sides with the children and punish one when they are fighting.

For some, these codes of conduct look familiar. If you polled parents or managers, many would say that dealing with conflict takes up a lot of time, and that it's a task they really don't enjoy. The problem is that they don't have a proactive, mutually agreed upon method to handle conflict. If there isn't a method in writing, then the unwritten code of conduct takes over.

Perhaps a written family code of conduct might look different. It might have some rules that Dad and/or Mom put in and some rules the children put in. Some might be made together. (This is not meant to sound old-fashioned. No one is suggesting that the family will become the Cleaver household of the 1950s.) But talking to one another and building a family communication contract, or a code of conduct, helps everyone to understand what the rules are so that they can live with respect for one another. It is particularly useful in blended family households.

A written code of conduct for families might look like this:

1) Kids can try to confront each other before bringing problems to Mom and Dad.

2) Parents will *not* take out frustration on the children.

3) If Dad is angry, he will tell us why and then make efforts to calm down.

4) We will speak up and say what is on our mind to each other.

5) We will encourage the children to work things out on their own, and if they can't, then we will intervene.

6) We will listen to the children without interrupting.

7) We will discuss decisions before rendering a verdict.

An example of a written code of conduct for a company could look like this:

1) Use positive communication and problem solving.

2) Agree to communicate directly, one to one.

3) Be receptive to positive confrontation.

4) Be aware of differing perspectives.

5) Check out perceptions for accuracy.

6) Direct others back to the source; don't participate in or listen to gossip.

Whether in a business or in a family, a code of conduct helps set the rules straight before people violate them, which enhances communication and strengthens relationships. Most people don't mind following rules if they are known in advance, if they are applied consistently, and if they are fair.

The following code of conduct was written by clients of mine who were separated and facing divorce. They were able to reconcile, and before moving back in together wrote this code of conduct. Printed here with permission.

Code of Conduct Agreement

This agreement is in the spirit of creating and maintaining a healthy relationship and a lifelong, happy marriage.

1. Communication: We agree to communicate in a respectful manner without blaming or accusing the other of wrongdoing. To communicate not only negative emotions or issues, but also positive thoughts, random thoughts, musings, and deep complex thoughts. We both need to feel that it is safe to communicate thoughts, needs, wants, likes, ideas and feelings without fear of judgment or retaliation.

2. Trust: We agree to trust one another, and to give the other the benefit of the doubt in all situations. We agree to practice the "innocent until proven guilty" motto. We also agree to be honest with each other in all of our communications.

3. Team: We agree to conduct ourselves as a team, and not one against the other. We agree to have each other's back, to stand up for one another, and believe that we are in this together. We agree to operate as teammates and not opposing entities that need to one up each other or delight in any "gotcha" moments. We agree to operate as two valuable team members who share the same goal of winning together as a team. We further agree that we will not discuss details of our personal life with other parties, or speak negatively of the other in front of others.

4. Compliments: We agree to verbalize things we like about the other. Remind each other what we love about the other person, what we like about them, point out their positive attributes, give pats on the back for a job well done, tell each other when they look nice, etc.

5. Arguing: We agree to stay in the present argument when we are arguing and not to drudge up shit from the past, or something from 5 years ago that has never been mentioned. It's okay to talk about these kinds of things, but not fair to bring them up during a current argument. We will stick to I statements, I feel...without blaming the other person. We agree that taking a "time out" is completely acceptable, however, the person in need of the time out will make the declaration that they need a time out, rather than just slamming a door and bolting out.

6. Compromise: Again, we are a team. We agree to allow one another to have it their way some times, and sometimes you'll get yours. It's give and take. Let me decide on a color, a picture, curtains, etc. And you can decide some things too. Let's not battle over every little thing, or put the other one down because they happen to like something different. Instead, we agree to take turns, share and compromise.

7. Compassion: Let's remember that we love each other. When the other is feeling down, sick, hurt, etc, the other partner agrees to show compassion and empathize with the other person. No blaming, even if there is a shred of responsibility, or one is in some way feeling the consequences of their behavior, etc., the other partner agrees to react with empathy when their partner is in need of emotional support. Whether it's with a hug or a verbalization of support, we agree that we will support one another through difficulties.

8. Fun: Let's have fun, make plans, do fun things with each other. We agree to go out for dinner at least once per week and to do a fun activity with each other once per week. This can be something as simple as staying at home and playing a game, or it can be something spontaneous or planned like taking swing dance lessons. We also agree that it is completely OK to have fun with others outside of our relationship. Go out with the girls/guys, etc.

9. Listening: We agree to listen while the other is speaking without interrupting, and to seek to understand the other before seeking to be understood.

10. 5-1 Rule/Positivity: Let's try to abide by this rule by having *5 or more positive interactions vs 1 negative one.* Make an effort to not be mean spirited or insulting to the other. Hold negative side comments or blaming statements, etc.

11. No yelling: We agree that we will not yell at each other...unless the house is on fire, or there is a tornado coming, or some sort of other disaster or an immediate threat of danger or harm.

12. Make joint decisions on important things: We agree to consult with one another on large purchases, investments, etc., so that we are both in agreement. No surprises. No coming home with a new 40K car, announcing that a large debt has just been paid off in a one lump sum, or that you've just loaned out 2K. Instead, we agree to consult, discuss and decide together as a team all financial decisions, and all decisions that might affect our relationship.

Are you asking me or telling?

My Dad used to say this phrase, and it didn't make sense to me until I was older. I think it is very useful for couples and parents with older children. If you are asking me, I will give you my opinion, if you are telling me, I will listen. Sometimes we don't listen to listen, but to solve your problem or give an opinion. Steven Covey once said, "We don't listen to understand but listen to reply."

Process vs goal orientation

Process is as important, if not more so, than the goal/outcome. If we have a relationship process as discussed in this book; dealing with perceptions, positive communication and problem solving outcomes usually take care of themselves.

Teeter-totter effect

Sometimes in a relationship partners consciously or unconsciously compensate for the other to keep things level. If one parent is more strict and the other more lenient, over time they get further apart as they attempt to compensate for the other. Likewise if one is depressed, seeks treatment and gets better the other partner could become depressed or act out to keep things the same. It's like announcing the new diet and your partner comes home tomorrow with ice cream!

3 things from self and 3 things from my partner

In couples counseling, not involving abuse or chemical dependency, partners are generally focused on what the other is doing (blame) to cause the problems. In order to re-focus each partner to what they have most control of (themselves) and what they want from the relationship, I ask the couple to write down 3 " things" they could do and 3 "things "they would like from their partner to make the relationship better. My colleague Harvey Kelber called this a Druthers list. I have the partners do this privately and bring it to the next session. What most couples find is what they could do differently is what their partner is asking for as well. They see that they are not so far apart and they have more in common than they thought.

Here is an example of 3 things from Jason and Ashely:

Jason for himself
- Watch some of my habits
- Make marriage and family a priority
- Time management

Ashely for Jason
- Decrease reckless behavior (weed/alcohol)
- Emphasize family more … others less
- Make time to talk to me

Ashely for herself
- Show more affection
- Don't over explain
- Time for Jeff alone

Jason for Ashely
- Be more affectionate
- Be less negative
- Let go of the past when together

If the couple is extremely polarized, I just ask for 3 "things" they could do, themselves, because they are so focused on blaming their partner and feeling like a victim. I frame it as "gut check" time. What are you willing to do or not do to try and save this relationship? Couples can do this at home as a starting point to jump start communication.

After using this technique for over 25 years, last night I had my first couple come for the second session where the husband stated, "I couldn't think of anything" (he was the one asking for a divorce). Needless to say, his wife was "crushed" and started to realize how checked out of the relationship he was.

Is this how you talk at home?

When I first see a couple or family and they are interrupting, arguing, blaming, not listening and generally not accepting much responsibility for their problems, I let it go on for a few minutes. Then I ask, "Is this how you all talk to each other at home?" As their eyes tilt towards the floor and they sheepishly utter, "yeah." I say, "How's that working for ya? Doesn't seem to be very productive to me, in fact it seems rather counterproductive! I'm guessing this is in part why you are here. You might want to consider learning a different way to communicate your concerns and solve problems." This gets their attention and moves the focus away from blaming each other.

Best gift for children especially in a divorce.

In a healthy relationship parents show love and respect to the other parent. Parents model how men and women in a healthy relationship are treated. In a relationship that is transitioning away from a two parent household, it is especially important to model social maturity. What you say about the other parent, you say about the child. When your children are grown up, what do you want them to say about how you handled the divorce? (See letter in Introduction.)

Pareto 80/20 rule

Named after Italian economist Vilfredo Pareto, who, while at the University of Lausanne in 1896, published his first paper "Cours d'économie politique." Essentially, Pareto showed that approximately 80% of the land in Italy was owned by 20% of the population; Pareto developed the principle by observing that 20% of the pea pods in his garden contained 80% of the peas. Pareto principle (also known as the 80–20 rule, the law of the vital few, and the principle of factor sparsity) states that, for many events, roughly 80% of the effects come from 20% of the causes. (Wikipedia 2016)

What do land ownership and peas have in common with relationships? Plenty! Couples and families can have multiple issues and feel overwhelmed, almost powerless to change themselves or their relationships. Rather than focus on "all the problems," if the focus is on going "back to basics 20%" on showing love, communicating respectfully, being honest and trusting, 80% of the issues get better.

Just like the chapters in this book, if we can be honest with ourselves, communicate respectfully, make our relations healthy and trust others, other things don't seem so overwhelming. It is the old principle of, " Give a man a fish, and you feed him for a day; show him how to catch fish, and you feed him for a lifetime." Take care of the basics and the rest get better.

Push-Me-Pull-You

Most couples/families that go to counseling have been experiencing problems for months (if not years). More often than not, each has "tried" at times to make a positive change, only to meet resistance from the other(s), who felt that they themselves have made efforts in the past that were not reciprocated. "Why should I try now? Where were you last month when I was making an effort?" This reminds me of the Push-Me-Pull-You Llama from *Dr. Doolittle*. It had two heads and two sets of front legs. When one half wanted to move forward, the other half would have to move backward. Most of the time, it just stood still with minimal progress.

Horse Race

In order to have a horse race, when the gates are opened, all the horses need to come out running as fast as they can to get to the finish line. It is the same with couples or families. This is where the "3 Thing" technique comes in. This can serve as the gate opening, and everyone needs to work as hard as possible to make a difference. If not, maybe that's saying something.

Takes two to think a joke is funny

I see some partners or family members who use sarcasm to make a point, and when called out they say, "I was only joking/kidding." For a joke to be funny, it takes two people to think it's funny. If only one person thinks it's funny, it's not a joke, and it needs to stop.

Although it takes two to have a relationship, it takes only one to change its quality.

How we act toward others often determines how they will react to us. If we don't like how someone is treating us, we have two choices. The first is to attempt to make the other person change. This is very difficult, especially if they don't want to change. The other choice is to change how we are acting. Often when we change the way we approach the other person, the other person will respond in a like manner.

Perhaps a different approach will change the reaction you are getting. Since we have the most control over ourselves, we must start by changing ourselves first. Remember, it doesn't take much to impact a relationship. When a subtle change is made by one of the parties, things have to change. Similarly, when one family member gets clean and sober, other family members have to change. (Fisher and Brown, 1992):

Teach a child or teen to be self-approving.

A social worker colleague, Diane Hockhammer, taught me to reframe praise for a child's behavior so the child can "own" the positive feelings. While it is always nice for a parent, counselor, adult or teacher to tell a child that they are proud of them or their behavior, in addition, you can take it one step further and say, "You must be really proud of yourself," or "I bet that feels really good to do that." That way the child learns to be self-approving rather than approval seeking. You can also amp it up by saying, "Man, if I did something like that, I would feel really good. You must feel really good about your bad self right now."

It's pretty cool to hear the kid say, "Yeah, I feel really good about what I did." As an adult there is usually not a long line of people waiting to tell us how wonderful we are. It really can be a do it yourself job if you have been taught how.

Consequences vs. deterrents.

I tell parents of teenagers taking away privileges, groundings or other forms of punishment are consequences not deterrents. Kids don't think, "I better be home on time to avoid being grounded or have my phone taken away." It is a consequence for a poor decision or choice. Consequences are important, don't get me wrong, but they don't have the impact parents think they do. In the United States some states have the death penalty for murder, but it doesn't stop people from killing each other.

Also be careful of limiting or withholding possible self-esteem building activities as a consequence. I hear parents all the time threaten to take away sports, lessons or some activity that is good for the kid. My partner Paul White, LCSW used to always give the example of the kid who is really good in English or Calculus, and the parent wouldn't say, "No more English or advanced math classes until your attitude is better, little Mister!"

Wouldn't want to be married to me.

I have always said I would not want to be married to me. I want to be in a relationship with someone who sees the world a little different than I do. I can profit from another set of "eyes or lens" to view the world. Value your differences! Make them work for you, not against you.

Algebra problem.

Just like in high school algebra class, the teacher always hounded the class to "show your work." Points were deducted even for a right answer if you didn't show your work. Partners and parents need to "show their work" too! How did they arrive at that conclusion? What thoughts or experiences did they have to help them reach that answer? Don't just do the work in your head and present the final answer. You need to talk it out so others can see how you got there! This is especially important for men.

—CHAPTER FIVE—

To Stay or Go ... or,
When is "Enough, *Enough?*"

CHAPTER FIVE

To Stay or Go … or, When is "Enough, *Enough?*"

The information provided here has stood the test of time in its value of being better for ourselves and others. Perhaps you will be able to use this in your daily life, pass it on to others and use it with friends and family.

Sometimes, no matter what you do, some people will not change or respond positively to your efforts. Some people in your solar system will just refuse to see anything differently and will continue to be dysfunctional. That's why I have included the following STAY OR GO … OR, WHEN IS "ENOUGH, *ENOUGH?*" section. This will give you a strategy to evaluate a job or a relationship and make an informed decision. Sometimes "going" is the healthiest decision you can make. But, doing so, as unfortunate as that may be, could be the best/only decision, and you need to see it that way. I know, I have done it and have seen many others make such decisions.

In dealing with others or evaluating anything, it is important — if not imperative — to have a mental strategy or structure. How do we approach a problem or situation? How do we know that we are evaluating it accurately? How can we best manage it if it's un-resolvable? When is enough, **enough**, and when do we need to get out or remove ourselves from the situation?

Whether we are evaluating a job or a relationship,

we need to do so in a systematic fashion so that if we elect to get out, we can do it with the confidence that we have tried everything else humanly possible. We want to avoid regret down the road from making a hasty or emotional decision. We want to avoid saying to ourselves, "If only I would have, could have or should have ..." As a rule of thumb, most problematic situations or relationships can be approached by asking the following three questions:

1. Can I impact the event?

2. Am I perceiving it or looking at it accurately?

3. Can I manage the stress associated with it?

The first question asks if you can impact the event, meaning, "What can you do to change the event?" If the event is a problem with a co-worker, supervisor, significant other or child, we need to ask ourselves, "What can I do (not what do they need to do) to change the event or problem?" If the problem is with a co-worker or supervisor, you could confront her, try to understand her perception, problem-solve, ask for help in resolving the problem or go to Human Resources or the next level of management. If the problematic event is with a family member or a significant relationship, you could try to talk about it, go for counseling, yell and scream about it, or try to ignore it or pull rank. Again, you need to ask yourself if you can go directly to the event to try to influence it and make it better. If you can, it may or may not work out for the better, but it may be better than complaining about it to all who will listen. Nor do you want to avoid dealing with it directly (enabling) or aggravate the event.

If you have tried to directly affect the event and the desired effect didn't occur, then you must ask yourself this question: "Do I stay or do I go?" Most of us at this point will elect to stay. If you do so, then the second step comes into play — asking yourself, "Am I looking at this situation accurately? How important is it? Can I or should I let it go?"

You need to examine your perceptions of the problematic event. Are you viewing it correctly? Are you guilty of viewing the event with one of the critical thinking errors mentioned earlier: (polarizing, awfulizing, over generalizing or breeding low self-esteem)? Separating out the events from perceptions and feelings is helpful when you're trying to identify your perception or view. Talking with a friend or professional (or reading about the problem) will help to give you a different perspective on the problem. If you are perceiving the event incorrectly, your perceptions can be changed to be more reflective of reality.

Sometimes, you need to ask yourself, "Just how important is it?" About seven out of 10 times, if you ask yourself that question and answer it honestly, you'll realize that the problem isn't that important. If it truly is important, then you need to deal with it. If your 15-year-old daughter gets decent grades, has minimal body piercings, she is involved in school activities and doesn't do drugs or alcohol, but her room is a disaster area, how much do you really want to argue about it? While it would be better if she were tidy, basically she is a pretty good kid; so maybe the messy room isn't that important after all.

In one of my consultations, I coached two people on the supervisory level (we'll call them Mary and Sue) who worked in an agency that provided services to a four-county region. Mary had a habit of asking Sue's staff to help her without first consulting Sue. Sue would become enraged, but would keep it all in, only to explode later. Sue's perception was that Mary did this because she didn't respect her, and that this behavior undermined her authority. They were supposed to be equals.

Sue requested a meeting. Mary stated that she didn't mean any disrespect, but that when she was short of help and Sue wasn't around, she didn't have time to find Sue. She felt that Sue was overly sensitive about this and needed to let it go.

Since Sue wanted to check out her perceptions, she wrote them down and consulted with a trusted colleague to see if he shared her perceptions. Since the mind can be an endless loop, if you just think about things to yourself, you will detour all over the place. Talking it over or writing it out makes it clearer. Sue did this, and thus entertained different ways of viewing the behavior of Mary: "Maybe she is just trying to get the job done. My people still respect me, so maybe my authority isn't undermined." After checking out the perceptions, Sue changed them.

When perceptions are accurate, you are faced with the decision again — do I stay or do I go? As Sue did in this instance, most people at this point elect to stay. If the perceptions are accurate and you cannot impact the event, then you must proceed to the next step, which asks, "Can I manage the stress?" (Besides, if you have developed the habit of eating and making mortgage payments, you may need to stay.)

If you elect to stay, there is a wealth of stress management information available today. The important thing is for people to actually USE something and not just make resolutions. Getting active and shifting the focus away from the event may help.

Sometimes, no matter what you do or try, it isn't enough to handle the stress. In this case, you are forced to make the last stay-or-go decision. At this point, many elect to go, or are asked to go, but will do so feeling like a failure. However, if you elect to go, it could be the healthiest choice for you. If you have tried to impact the event, evaluated your perceptions, and attempted to manage your stress to no avail, then maybe going is the most positive thing to do. The alternative may be to become bitter and unpleasant, which is toxic to yourself and those around you.

—CONCLUSION—

Conclusion

Many people might mistakenly think that the techniques spoken of here are processes for problem relationships only. Even in a healthy family, the ability to understand, communicate, solve problems and enhance relationships is not easy. Although these processes are used in problem relationships, they also can be used in other situations. When an organizational merger or acquisition creates a need to blend two different cultures, these processes can help. They also can be used in a downsizing situation that leaves the new corporate culture significantly different from the old, thus creating mixed feelings among remaining employees who may need some type of intervention to adjust to the new culture.

Growing up, most of us did not intentionally study effective ways to communicate or deal with conflict. We learned from our parents, family members, friends or significant others who themselves may not have been the most effective communicators. Families, parents, children and spouses don't come with owner's manuals, and there is not necessarily a right way or wrong way to do things. As we grow and mature in life and in our relationships, we acquire our own styles of interacting with those closest to us. We adopt these methods mostly through trial and error, and they may be effective or not. We may discover what we don't want to do but not find what we want to do.

Sometimes it is more difficult to understand and communicate with those closest to us, because our feelings get in the way. This book presents a true strategy or game plan on how to have quality relationships with others.

I once heard someone tell the story of a trip he had taken. To keep his child occupied, he took a picture of the world from a travel magazine, tore it up into pieces and told the small child to "put together this puzzle of the world." The child had the puzzle put together in seconds. When the man asked his child how she completed it so quickly, the child said, "On the other side of the world was a picture of person, so I just put the eyes, and nose, and mouth where they were supposed to go."

The moral is to put together the person, and the world takes care of itself.

Thanks for stopping by.

Peace,
Norm

AFTER 40 YEARS IN THERAPY, WHAT HAVE LEARNED?
Bibliography

Bartz, Wayner & Rasor, Richard A. *Surviving with Kids*. NY, Ballantine Books, 1978.

Bramson, Robert M. PhD. *Coping with Difficult People*. NY, Ballantine Books, 1981.

Burns, David D. MD. *Feeling Good: The New Mood Therapy*. NY, Avon Books, 1999.

Conner, Daryl R. *Managing at the Speed of Change*. NY, Villard Books, 1994.

Conners, Roger & Smith Tom. *Change the Culture Change the Game*. NY, Penguin Books, 2011

Corsini, Raymond, ed. *Current Psychotherapies*. Itasca, IL, F.E. Peacock Publishers, Inc., 1973.

Covey, Stephen R. *The Seven Habits of Highly Effective People*. NY, Fireside Books, 1989.

Dasenbrook, Norman C. LCPC & Mastroianni, Michael M. MAT. *Harnessing the Power of Conflict*. IL. Cysand, 2003

Dasenbrook, Norman C. LCPC. *Complete Guide to Private Practice*. IL. Crysand 2015

Ellis, Albert Ph.D. *A Guide to Rational Living*. NY, Whilsire Books, 1997

Ellis, Albert (2001). *Overcoming Destructive Beliefs, Feelings, and Behaviors: New Directions for Rational Emotive Behavior Therapy*. Prometheus Books.

Fisher, Roger & Ury, William. *Getting to Yes*. NY, Penguin Books, 1991.

Gladwell, Malcom. *The Tipping Point*. NY, Little Brown, 2000.

Fisher, Roger & Brown, Scott. *Getting Together*. NY, Penguin Books, 1988.

Gordon, Dr. Thomas. P.E.T. *Parent Effectiveness Training*. NY, Wyden, Inc., 1975.

Leadership Advantage. *The Business Case for Coaching*. 2001

Morin, William. Viewpoint: *Six Common Beliefs of Executives Who Fail*. Columns, Dec. 2002

Pastor, Larry M.D. "Single Session Therapy Effective in the Workplace" *Psychiatric Times*, Jul. 1993.

Ury, William. *Getting Past No*. NY, Bantam Books, 1993.

Weisinger, Hendrie. *Emotional Intelligence at Work*. San Francisco, Josey-Bass,1998.

Weiss, Donald. *Effective Team Building*. NY, Amacom (American Management Association), 1993.

Weiss, Donald. *Conflict Resolution*. NY, Amacom (American Management Association), 1993.

https://en.wikipedia.org/wiki/Rational_emotive_behavior_therapy#cite_note-ellis1-11

AFTER 40 YEARS IN THERAPY, WHAT HAVE LEARNED?
AUTHOR BIOGRAPHY

Norman C. Dasenbrook, MS, LCPC

Norman C. Dasenbrook, MS, LCPC is a Licensed Clinical Professional Counselor who has over 40 years' experience in the fields of mental health, consulting, business and alternative dispute resolution processes. Norm's professional experience includes working in community mental health serving the chronic mentally ill, clinical director and owner of a substance abuse center, employee assistance program provider, divorce mediator and collaborative law professional, organizational consultant, executive coach, trainer, author and private practice counselor treating teens, adults, couples and families.

Norm is Past President of the Illinois Mental Health Counselors Association, served on the Governing Council for the Illinois Counseling Association and winner of the Distinguished Service Award. He served as a consultant to the American Counseling Association on Private Practice Issues. He is a member of American Counseling Association, American Mental Health Counselors Association, Illinois Counseling Association and Illinois Mental Health Counseling Association.

Norm offers presentations on this book and has been presenting his workshop, "Starting,

Maintaining and Expanding a Successful Private Practice: Surviving or Thriving?" nationally for over 18 years. He has authored the leading book on private practice, "The Complete Guide to Private Practice for Licensed Mental Health Professionals". Norm also provides practice consultation and coaching. (www.counseling-privatepractice.com)

Through his consulting company Crysand Consulting he serves as an organizational consultant, trainer and executive coach for improved performance and interpersonal skills for organizations (www.crysand.com). Norm is also co-author of *Harnessing the Power of Conflict: Optimum Performance Through the Self-Mediation Method*, 1994, Crysand Press, *Harnessing the Power of Conflict: Business and Family,* 1997, Crysand Press and *Harnessing the Power of Conflict: Leading, Learning and Living*, 2003, Crysand Press.